A-LEVEL YEAR 2

STUDENT GUIDE

D0230898

EDEXCEL

Psychology

Applications of psychology

Christine Brain

PHILIP ALLAN FOR

HODDER
EDUCATION

AN HACHETTE UK C

Philip Allan, an imprint of Hodder Education, an Hachette UK company, Blenheim Court, George Street, Banbury, Oxfordshire OX16 5BH

Orders

Bookpoint Ltd, 130 Milton Park, Abingdon, Oxfordshire OX14 4SB

tel: 01235 827827

fax: 01235 400401

e-mail: education@bookpoint.co.uk

Lines are open 9.00 a.m.–5.00 p.m., Monday to Saturday, with a 24-hour message answering service. You can also order through the Hodder Education website: www.hoddereducation.co.uk

© Christine Brain 2016

ISBN 978-1-4718-5940-3

First printed 2016

Impression number 5 4 3 2 1

Year 2020 2019 2018 2017 2016

This Guide has been written specifically to support students preparing for the Edexcel A-level Psychology examinations. The content has been neither approved nor endorsed by Edexcel and remains the sole responsibility of the author.

Typeset by Integra Software Services Pvt. Ltd., Pondicherry, India

Cover photograph: agsandrew/Fotolia

Printed in Italy

Hachette UK's policy is to use papers that are natural, renewable and recyclable products and made from wood grown in sustainable forests. The logging and manufacturing processes are expected to conform to the environmental regulations of the country of origin.

Contents

■ Getting the most from this book

Exam-style questions

Commentary on the questions

Tips on what you need to do to gain full marks, indicated by the icon **e**

Sample student answers

Practise the questions, then look at the student answers that follow.

Commentary on sample student answers

Find out how many marks each answer would be awarded in the exam and then read the comments (preceded by the icon **e**) following each student answer.

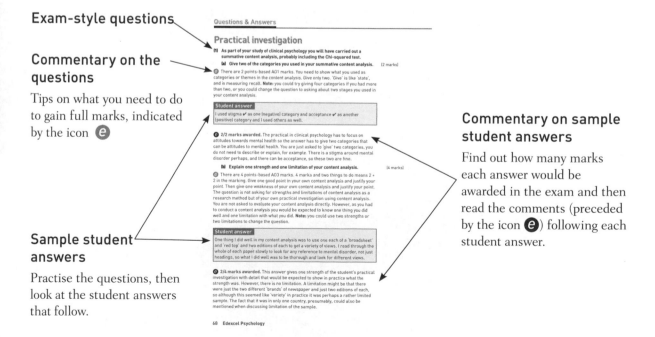

Questions & Answers

Practical investigation

(1) As part of your study of clinical psychology you will have carried out a summative content analysis, probably including the Chi-squared test.

(a) Give two of the categories you used in your summative content analysis. [2 marks]

e There are 2 points-based AO1 marks. You need to show what you used as categories or themes in the content analysis. Give only two. 'Give' is like 'state', and is measuring recall. **Note:** you could try giving four categories if you had more than two, or you could change the question to asking about two stages you used in your content analysis.

Student answer

I used stigma ✔ as one (negative) category and acceptance ✔ as another (positive) category and I used others as well.

e 2/2 marks awarded. The practical in clinical psychology has to focus on attitudes towards mental health so the answer has to give two categories that can be attitudes to mental health. You are just asked to 'give' two categories, you do not need to describe or explain, for example. There is a stigma around mental disorder perhaps, and there can be acceptance, so these two are fine.

(b) Explain one strength and one limitation of your content analysis. [4 marks]

e There are 4 points-based AO3 marks. 4 marks and two things to do means 2 + 2 in the marking. Give one good point in your own content analysis and justify your point. Then give one weakness of your own content analysis and justify your point. The question is not asking for strengths and limitations of content analysis as a research method but of your own practical investigation using content analysis. You are not asked to evaluate your content analysis directly. However, as you had to conduct a content analysis you would be expected to know one thing you did well and one limitation with what you did. **Note:** you could use two strengths or two limitations to change the question.

Student answer

One thing I did well in my content analysis was to use one each of a 'broadsheet' and 'red top' and two editions of each to get a variety of views. I read through the whole of each paper slowly to look for any reference to mental disorder, not just headings, so what I did well was to be thorough and look for different views.

e 2/4 marks awarded. This answer gives one strength of the student's practical investigation with detail that would be expected to show in practice what the strength was. However, there is no limitation. A limitation might be that there were just the two different 'brands' of newspaper and just two editions of each, so although this seemed like 'variety' in practice it was perhaps a rather limited sample. The fact that it was in only one country, presumably, could also be mentioned when discussing limitation of the sample.

68 Edexcel Psychology

■ About this book

This guide covers the applications of the Edexcel GCE AS and A-level Psychology 2015 specification. It covers Topic 5 Clinical psychology (the compulsory application), and looks at Topics 6, 7 and 8 (three other 'option' applications, from which you must choose one). These are examined in A-level Paper 2 and to an extent in A-level Paper 3.

Table 1 shows how these papers fit in the overall AS and A-level qualifications. AS Papers 1 and 2 cover Topics 1 to 4, and is Year 1 of the A level. A-level Paper 1 examines the four topics from Year 1 with the addition of issues and debates. A-level Paper 2 covers applications of psychology with the addition of issues and debates. A-level Paper 3 covers psychological skills, including specifically the method, studies and issues and debates from the A-level course.

- Student Guide 1 covers the first two topic areas in Year 1 of the A level, which make up half the AS (social and cognitive psychology).
- Student Guide 2 covers the last two topic areas in Year 1 of the A level, which make up the other half of the AS (biological psychology and learning theories).
- Student Guide 3 covers Topics 5 to 8 (clinical, criminological, child and health psychology), which are examined in the A-level Paper 2.
- Student Guide 4 covers Topic 9 (method, studies and issues and debates), which is examined in A-level Paper 3.

Table 1 Overview of AS and A-level Papers (**bold** indicates covered in this guide)

AS	A-level Year 1	A-level Year 2
Paper 1: social, cognitive	Paper 1: social, cognitive, biological, learning (including issues and debates)	Paper 2: **clinical** and one from **criminological**, **child** and **health** (including issues and debates)
Paper 2: biological, learning	Paper 3: psychological skills (method, studies, issues and debates)	

Aims

This guide is not a textbook — there is no substitute for reading the required material and taking notes. Nor does it tell you the actual questions on your paper. The aim of this guide is to provide you with a clear understanding of the requirements of A-level Paper 2 and to an extent A-level Paper 3, and to advise you on how best to meet these requirements. This guide looks at:

- the psychology you need to know about
- what you need to be able to do and what skills you need
- how you could go about learning the necessary material
- what is being examined, including mathematical skills
- what you should expect in the examination
- how you could tackle the different styles of exam question
- the format of the exam, including what questions might look like
- how questions might be marked, including examples of answers, with examiner's comments

How to use this guide

A good way of using this guide is to read it through in the order in which it is presented. Alternatively, you can consider each topic in the Content Guidance section, and then turn to a relevant question in the Questions & Answers section. Whichever way you use the guide, try some of the questions yourself to test your learning.

You will cover clinical psychology, which accounts for 54 of the 90 marks available in A-level Paper 2, or 60% of the paper. You will then choose one from the other three applications (options). All three of these option applications are briefly touched on in the Content Guidance section of this guide.

In the Questions & Answers section there is a clinical psychology section, which includes an issues and debates question, and an option application section, which will offer guidance on the application you choose.

Questions & Answers

Note that cross-references in the Content Guidance are given to answers in the Questions & Answers section that provide more information on particular areas of content.

Glossary

A list of terms is included at the end of this guide (pages 83–86). They are organised alphabetically and subdivided into the four topic areas — clinical, criminological, child and health psychology. This list of definitions can help you in your revision. You could go through the Glossary matching terms to topic areas, for example, or picking out all the methodology terms to draw them together.

Content Guidance

■ Clinical psychology

This section looks at clinical psychology with its five main parts (content; methods; studies; key question; practical investigation). In some places in your course you can choose what you study. In this section suitable material is presented, but you may have studied different examples. *You might be better advised to revise the material you chose for your course.*

Table 1 Summary of clinical psychology in your course

Content
The four 'D's relating to diagnosis of mental health; the DSM (DSM IV-TR or DSM-5) and ICD classification systems and reliability and validity of diagnosis. Symptoms and features of schizophrenia; neurotransmitters as an explanation of schizophrenia; one other biological explanation, and one non-biological explanation. Symptoms and features of one of unipolar depression, OCD and anorexia nervosa, with one biological and one non-biological explanation of one of these disorders. Two treatments, one biological and one psychological, for schizophrenia. Two treatments, one biological and one psychological, for one of unipolar depression, OCD or anorexia nervosa. In this guide, unipolar depression is chosen as the 'other' disorder
Individual differences such as in cultural effects relating to diagnoses and mental disorders.
Developmental psychology such as biological and non-biological explanations of schizophrenia.
Methodology
HCPC guidelines for clinical practitioners; researching mental health, including longitudinal, cross-sectional, cross-cultural, and meta-analytic designs, also primary and secondary data. The use of case studies and one example (here Lavarenne et al., 2013, is chosen) and the use of interviews and one example (here Vallentine et al., 2010, is chosen). You also need to cover analysis of quantitative data using descriptive and inferential statistics, drawing on Year 1 learning, as well as analysis of qualitative data using thematic analysis from Year 1 and also using grounded theory.
One classic study and two studies in detail
Rosenhan (1973) is the classic study and Carlsson et al. (2000) is the required study for schizophrenia. You then need one from a choice of two focusing on your chosen disorder. For depression, the 'other' disorder chosen here, Williams et al. (2013) is described and evaluated. You may have studied Kroenke et al. (2008) instead, or you may have chosen a different disorder with its related studies.
Key issue
The issue of mental health in the workplace is given here, but you may have looked at one or more different key questions.
Practical
You will have carried out at least one practical within clinical psychology and you should use your own investigation, because you will have 'learned by doing'. Some ideas about the practical are suggested in this guide.

Questions & Answers

Clinical psychology Overview Q1 describes what is meant by clinical psychology. What follows is a brief summary.

Clinical psychology is about explaining and treating mental health issues and different treatments such as drug therapy or counselling perhaps using cognitive–behavioural therapy (CBT).

Diagnosis of mental disorders

Mental disorders can be diagnosed using four 'D's, which are **danger**, **distress**, **dysfunction** and **deviance**.

Questions & Answers

Clinical psychology Content Q1 defines the four terms that are the four 'D's: danger, distress, dysfunction and deviance.

Exam tip

Be ready to give examples to help to explain deviance, dysfunction, distress and danger. A disorder can be diagnosed if someone is a danger to themselves, shows deviant behaviour which is dysfunctional for them and if they are distressed, for example. Give real examples for each of these issues.

Table 2 Strengths and weaknesses of the four 'D's of diagnosis

Strengths	Weaknesses
Using the four 'D's can work for professionals and has a practical application in that all the features are recognisable and can be measured without a lot of training, including using them alongside the DSM	There can be subjectivity in the use of the four 'D's. If professionals do not agree, this suggests a lack of **reliability** too
Davis (2009) shows how using danger, distress, dysfunction and deviance has **validity** in that they are found in cases of mental disorder — a disorder affects someone's life (dysfunction) and can include behaviour against the norm and not approved of (deviance)	Davis (2009) suggested a fifth 'D' was useful — 'duration' — as the length of time of a difficulty (such as distress or dysfunction) is important in diagnosis. Some small amount of distress or dysfunction can be 'normal' in some situations, for example. If it goes on, it might be seen as less 'normal'

Links

Individual differences link

Diagnosis can depend on the individual, in that what is distressing for one person might be less distressing for another and what someone would find dysfunctional might not affect someone else so much. Whether something is dysfunctional can depend on someone's job, for example, and the degree to which a person is distressed can depend on their level of support. Stress is found when someone believes they do not have the resources to cope, and that is an individual belief.

Exam tip

Learning evaluation points can help your understanding of material and revision can be helped by focusing on the strengths and weaknesses of studies, theories and concepts. Be sure to note some strengths and weaknesses for all that you have to cover in your course.

Exam tip

You will need to know about individual differences (and developmental psychology) in clinical psychology, as in other content in your course. Make notes about this area, ready for any questions that focus on individual differences or developmental issues.

Knowledge check 1

Using nicotine addiction as a disorder, give examples of danger, dysfunction, distress and deviance related to its diagnosis.

Classification systems, including reliability and validity

Two classification systems are the **DSM** and the ICD. The DSM you need to study is either DSM-IV-TR or DSM-5. The current ICD version is the ICD-10, though another version is expected in 2018.

The DSM

The *Diagnostic and Statistical Manual of Mental Disorders* (DSM), published by the American Psychiatric Association (APA), is from the USA but can be used elsewhere. The DSM-I was published in 1952. The DSM-IV was published in 1994. There was a revision after that (DSM IV(r)) and then a 'text revision' version in 2000 (DSM-IV-TR).

Table 3 The DSM

DSM-IV-TR (published in 2000)	DSM-5 (published in May 2013)
Has five axes: Axis I: clinical, major mental, developmental and learning disorders needing immediate attention from a clinician Axis II: underlying personality conditions and mental retardation Axis III: general medical conditions such as diabetes or a heart condition Axis IV: psychosocial and environmental factors Axis V: assessing someone's overall functioning such as rating their coping with life	Section I: explains how the DSM-5 is organised and the changes from the DSM-IV-TR Section II: all of the mental disorders are listed in chapters, including schizophrenia spectrum and other psychiatric disorders in one, and bipolar and related disorders in another Section III: covers emerging measures and models, looking to the future of diagnosis. Can mean culture is taken into account, and new diagnoses before they are ready for Section II (such as internet gaming disorder)

Table 4 Strengths and weaknesses of the DSM (both DSM-IV-TR and DSM-5)

Strengths	Weaknesses
The DSM allows a common diagnosis by clinicians which without such a classification system would not be possible	The DSM 'medicalises' people, seeing them as patients and prescribing treatment. However, Laing suggests schizophrenia is another way of living rather than a medical illness
Studies have found reliability in the DSM. E.g. Goldstein (1988) found the DSM-III to be reliable in that clinicians using it came up with the same diagnosis for individuals. The DSM-5 used trials to test its reliability where clinicians independently assessed the same patient and reliability was found	There can be criticism of the DSM regarding social norms being reflected in judgements about what a disorder is. For example, the British Psychological Society (BPS) has criticised the DSM-5 as requiring **subjective** judgements about symptoms

Reliability of the DSM

Reliability relates to whether one person's set of symptoms would receive a different diagnosis from different physicians. If a different diagnosis is given, leading to different treatment suggestions, treatment might not work. Diagnoses need to be reliable.

Table 5 Studies relating to the reliability of the DSM

Study	Evidence regarding reliability of the DSM
Goldstein (1988)	Using the DSM-III, Goldstein re-diagnosed patients originally diagnosed using the DSM-II, and found similarities in diagnosis. She also asked experts to do the same using a **single-blind technique**. There was a high level of agreement and **inter-rater reliability**. The DSM-IV-TR built on the DSM-III and so is likely to be reliable too, as is the DSM-5
Kirk and Kutchins (1992)	Kirk and Kutchins argued that interviewing and using questionnaires to test for reliability in the DSM did not relate to real settings, and that often interviewers and researchers were not trained correctly, so reliability, even though found, is in doubt (up to 1992)

Table 6 Strengths and weaknesses regarding reliability of diagnosis using the DSM

Strengths	Weaknesses
Brown et al. (2001): two independent interviews were carried out on each of 362 patients with good reliability in the diagnosis of anxiety disorders	It is possible that studies use clinicians to check reliability of diagnoses who have had similar training and have similar views about disorders, so when they are used to check someone else's diagnosis there is similarity in the diagnosis. This might just mean that their subjectivity is the same as those who did the original diagnosis. Perhaps this is more about validity than reliability, but could be seen as a weakness
Studies have found reliability in the DSM, e.g. Goldstein (1988) as explained in Table 5. The DSM-5 used trials to test its reliability	Kirk and Kutchins (1992) argued that interviewing and questionnaires were used in research situations to check diagnosis using more than one clinician and that those gathering the data were not that well trained, as well as the setting being artificial

Validity of the DSM

Validity relates to whether what is measured measures what it claims to measure. If a diagnosis of schizophrenia did not measure schizophrenia, and treatment was planned according to that diagnosis, treatment presumably would not work. A diagnosis needs to be valid to be useful. If the DSM was not reliable it would not be valid either, because it would mean different clinicians diagnosing different disorders in the same person, so not predicting the course of a disorder in real life.

> **Exam tip**
>
> In your course you are asked to know about internal validity, predictive validity and ecological validity, so be ready to discuss those particular types of validity. Predictive validity is mentioned in the text here, for example.

> **Exam tip**
>
> It is useful to know studies so that you have evidence, such as for the reliability of the DSM. Where possible when revising, look for such evidence and aim to used named evidence in exam answers when relevant (such as when evaluating).

> **Knowledge check 2**
>
> Use Kirk and Kutchins' (1992) criticism of studies claiming reliability for the DSM to evaluate the findings of Brown et al. (2001).

Table 7 Studies relating to the validity of the DSM

Study	Evidence regarding validity of the DSM
Kim-Cohen et al. (2005)	The study looked at the behaviour of children diagnosed with conduct disorder to see whether those children were more likely to report their own antisocial behaviour and to be disruptive during assessment. These behaviours would be expected if their diagnosis was valid. The results of the study did find validity in the diagnosis
Lee (2006)	Teacher opinion about a child was compared with an ADHD diagnosis using the DSM-IV-TR. It was found that there was a match between the measures, so the DSM was valid. However, boys fit the DSM criteria better than girls

Table 8 Strengths and weaknesses regarding validity of diagnosis using the DSM

Strengths	Weaknesses
When validity is tested, different diagnoses such as conduct disorder and ADHD are looked at and still validity is found. This strengthens the findings. Also, different research methods are used such as **interviews** and questionnaires, including asking teachers	The DSM does not suit co-morbidity that well. It homes in on one diagnosis and does not do well for people with multiple issues regarding their mental health
Studies have found reliability in the DSM, e.g. Goldstein (1988) as explained in Table 5. The DSM-5 used trials to test its reliability where clinicians independently assessed the same patient and reliability was found. If there is reliability, then there is validity	Some mental disorders are known by their symptoms by many people not just clinicians. A teacher might use the symptoms and features of ADHD to describe a child they know who 'has that label'. So teacher descriptions and DSM diagnosis are likely to match as the DSM has informed people about ADHD and vice versa

Knowledge check 3

Define predictive validity, internal validity and ecological validity and aim to relate them to validity of diagnosis.

The ICD

The ICD is a World Health Organisation (WHO) classification system and is the *International Statistical Classification of Diseases and Related Health Problems*. It is used more than the DSM across the world. The ICD-10 (the latest edition — the ICD-11 is expected in 2018) goes up to XXII categories. Mental and behavioural disorders are number V and diseases of the nervous system are number VI.

Table 9 Strengths and weaknesses of the reliability of the ICD-10, using schizophrenia as an example

Strengths	Weaknesses
Jakobsen et al. (2005) found reliability when comparing the ICD-10 and the DSM, as did Hiller et al. (1992) when comparing the ICD-10 with the DSM-III-R. There is evidence, which is a strength	Cheniaux et al. (2009) found the ICD-10 to be more reliable than the DSM-IV when diagnosing schizophrenia, so there could be some lack of reliability (as there are differences in diagnosis between the two)
When studies find reliability they test for inter-rater reliability in their findings, which gives a quantitative measure of how reliable a diagnostic system is	The reliability figures were around 0.50, which leaves a lack of agreement too

Exam tip

You can use evidence from studies to evaluate the reliability or validity of a diagnosis or diagnosis system. You can also evaluate the studies themselves as an extension point.

Table 10 Strengths and weaknesses of the validity of the ICD-10, using schizophrenia as an example

Strengths	Weaknesses
Pihlajamaa et al. (2008) compared the ICD-10, DSM-IV and the DSM-III-R using people diagnosed with core schizophrenia spectrum disorders (in Finland). Diagnoses corresponded around 70% of the time and it was concluded that diagnoses were valid	Jansson et al. (2002) found the ICD-9 and ICD-10 focused on different features and symptoms (schizophrenia), which means lack of validity
Jansson et al. (2002) also found validity (in Copenhagen). This time data were gathered using interviewing and assessments. The ICD-10 and the DSM-IV gave the best agreement regarding diagnosis (0.823), which suggests validity	A problem is with the complexity of disorders such as separating schizophrenia from schizoaffective disorder. Ellason and Ross (1995) suggested those diagnosed with dissociative identity disorder suit features and symptoms of schizophrenia more than those diagnosed with schizophrenia (looking at positive symptoms)

Schizophrenia: symptoms, features and explanations

Symptoms and features

Features

Schizophrenia is found in about 1% of the population. Its main feature is **psychosis**, which, unlike **neurosis**, means mental health issues that separate the person from reality. It tends to be diagnosed in adolescence but can be diagnosed at any age up to around 30 years old.

Symptoms

Schizophrenia is characterised using first- and second-rank symptoms or positive and negative symptoms.

- First-rank symptoms include hearing voices and feeling someone else is telling you what to do.
- Second-rank symptoms include having emotions that do not fluctuate.
- Positive symptoms are behaviours that can be noted, such as delusions and hallucinations, and include first-rank symptoms.
- Negative symptoms are when normal functioning is not there, such as not having variation in emotions or having speech problems.

Hallucinations involve seeing people and things that are not there and **delusions** are false beliefs, such as someone thinking their movements are controlled by someone else. **Thought insertion** is someone thinks their thoughts are put there by someone else and **disordered thinking** is when someone finds it hard to think in an ordered and logical way to make them make sense.

Neurotransmitters as an explanation

Neurotransmitters are chemicals in the brain that are involved in messaging. Excess **dopamine** and **glutamate** functioning are two neurotransmitter explanations for schizophrenia.

Exam tip

Be ready to define terms for 2 or 3 marks. Prepare examples, which will also help your understanding. You could go through the clinical psychology section, write out all the terms (including those in the headings) and prepare a definition that would get you 3 marks.

Knowledge check 4

What is meant by 'feature' and what is meant by 'symptom' of schizophrenia? Use one example for each.

Table 11 Strengths and weaknesses of the dopamine hypothesis to explain schizophrenia

Strengths	Weaknesses
People given Levodopa, which adds to dopamine production, for Parkinson's disease can experience schizophrenia-like symptoms, suggesting excess dopamine has a role in schizophrenia	PET scans show that blocking dopamine using drugs does not reduce the symptoms for patients who have had schizophrenia for 10+ years, though if given earlier more than 90% of patients respond
Scanning shows giving amphetamines to people with schizophrenia leads to more dopamine being released than in those without schizophrenia, giving evidence that dopamine is involved in the disorder	Amphetamines produce only positive symptoms of schizophrenia (increasing dopamine), so there must be more to it and the dopamine hypothesis does not explain negative symptoms

Questions & Answers

Clinical psychology Content Q2 covers the strengths of the neurotransmitter explanation of schizophrenia and there is some discussion of using evidence from Carlsson et al. (2000), the required study for schizophrenia.

Table 12 Strengths and weaknesses of the glutamate hypothesis to explain schizophrenia

Strengths	Weaknesses
The glutamate hypothesis works with the dopamine hypothesis and expands on it so the evidence for the dopamine hypothesis is included, giving strength to the idea and adding a body of knowledge	Animal studies may show erratic behaviour which is identified as similar to schizophrenia and psychosis. However, generalising from animal studies to humans is difficult
Evidence from **neuroimaging** and animal studies shows that blocking glutamate relates to psychotic symptoms such as negative affect and the findings from different research methods support one another, suggesting reliability. See Carlsson et al. (2000)	Using scanning in humans might not yield valid data as humans being researched are likely to be stressed and not in a 'normal' frame of mind. Their brain functioning is likely to be affected and 'different' in any case

Exam tip

You could use index cards with a term on one side and an explanation on the other to help your learning and you can draw up the cards using the Glossary. Then sort the terms into the sections of your course (you could use colours to separate them).

Another biological explanation: genes

There is evidence from twin and family studies for a genetic explanation of schizophrenia. If a family has more members than usual with schizophrenia, that suggests a genetic link. Similarly, if identical (**monozygotic** or **MZ**) twins share schizophrenia more than non-identical (**dizygotic** or **DZ**) twins, again that suggests a genetic link.

Exam tip

Carlsson et al. (2000), the study for schizophrenia in your course, focuses on neurotransmitter functioning and the glutamate hypothesis as an explanation for schizophrenia. Use the study for information about this part of your course.

Knowledge check 5

Drawing on what you learned in biological psychology, explain neurotransmitter functioning by explaining how drugs can 'block' dopamine functioning.

Table 13 Studies relating to a genetic explanation of schizophrenia

Study	Evidence regarding genetic explanation of schizophrenia
Gottesman and Shields (1966)	The study showed a concordance (agreement) rate for MZ twins regarding schizophrenia of between 35% and 58% and for DZ twins between 9% and 26%. For MZ twins around 42% of the time both have schizophrenia and for DZ twins the incidence is an average of about 17%
Sullivan et al. (2003, cited in Tiwari et al., 2010)	From a meta-analysis they found a figure of 81% heritability, which is high, but which Tiwari et al. (2010) say is similar to recent findings, such as Lichtenstein et al.'s (2009) figure of about 64% heritability

> **Exam tip**
>
> It is useful to prepare evidence for all statements you make, including, where possible, strengths and weaknesses. This means making notes about what research has found. 'Names' are good if you can remember them, as are numbers/results.

> **Knowledge check 6**
>
> What does it mean to say there is a 64% heritability figure (Lichtenstein et al., 2009)?

A non-biological explanation

Another explanation is the social causation hypothesis with a focus on environmental factors explaining schizophrenia.

> **Exam tip**
>
> When considering explanations for a mental disorder, focusing on biological causes for one explanation and social or environmental causes for the other is often what is done. This is like focusing on nature and nurture, which is one way to help you to remember two explanations, such as for schizophrenia.

> **Knowledge check 7**
>
> Explain how social drift shows how those with schizophrenia are found in lower social classes and in poverty, so social situation is not a cause but a result of the disorder.

Table 14 Strengths and weaknesses of the social causation/environmental cause of schizophrenia

Strengths	Weaknesses
Twin studies suggest a heritability element for schizophrenia but it is not 100%. This suggests an environmental cause too and social causation helps to explain what such environmental effects might be	Diagnosis might be the problem as those in inner-city areas, living alone, unemployed, living in poverty might be diagnosed more as having schizophrenia
Evidence suggests an environmental aspect to schizophrenia such as found in Brown's (2010) review	Being in socially adverse conditions might be the result of schizophrenia, which makes holding down a job, for example, hard. Social position might not be an explanation, it might be a result

> **Exam tip**
>
> When explaining the strengths and weaknesses of an explanation, aim to explain fully. This is not always done in this brief guide, but in an exam answer there needs to be a full explanation of each point made.

Links

Developmental psychology link

If schizophrenia is caused by social adversity in some way then that suggests that it is people's environment and experiences that cause schizophrenia, which is about their development.

Unipolar depression: symptoms, features and two explanations

Depression is chosen here but you may have covered obsessive–compulsive disorder (OCD) or anorexia nervosa.

Exam tip

In looking at explanations of unipolar depression, neurotransmitter functioning is considered here and drug therapy is a suggested therapy. You can make links with neurotransmitter functioning explanations of schizophrenia and drug therapy for schizophrenia because the functioning is the same.

Symptoms and features of unipolar depression

Unipolar depression is characterised by sadness, disappointment, loneliness, self-doubt and hopelessness. Symptoms include irritability, lethargy, lack of concentration and loss of interest in things. Features include that it is common in a society. At any one time between 5% and 9% of women and from 2% to 3% of men will be clinically depressed.

One biological explanation of unipolar depression

Neurotransmitter functioning, specifically low levels of serotonin, can explain depression. The monoamine hypothesis is that depression comes from a decrease in monoamine neurotransmitters such as serotonin and noradrenaline.

Table 15 Strengths and weaknesses of the monoamine hypothesis for unipolar depression

Strengths	Weaknesses
Haase and Brown (2015) and Delgado (2000) claim that if drugs that replace monoamine deficiencies work with depression then that is evidence for the monoamine depletion explanation	Some drugs work at the glutamate receptors (Palucha and Pilc, 2005), so it seems that it is not just monoamines at work in depression
Animal studies support the idea that depression comes from low levels of monoamines, as does scanning (see Krishnan and Nestler's (2008) review of methods used)	SSRIs do not help everyone with depression (Haase and Brown, 2015), so lack of serotonin seems not to be a complete explanation (SSRIs add to serotonin levels)

One non-biological explanation of unipolar depression

Just as with schizophrenia, social factors are seen as important in depression. Social issues such as lack of social support have been suggested as causes of unipolar depression. Brown et al. (1986) found that social support was important in preventing depression, linking to the idea that social isolation is involved in schizophrenia.

Links

Developmental psychology link

Having social support (or not having it) is part of our experience and that is part of how we develop.

Exam tip

Be sure to learn both symptoms and features and to know the difference. When reading an exam question, focus on exactly what is asked for. You might be asked for features or symptoms separately.

Exam tip

You learned about neurotransmitter functioning in biological psychology, so draw on that understanding when looking at the neurotransmitter explanation for both schizophrenia and depression — but note the different neurotransmitters and some differences in processing.

Exam tip

You only need one non-biological theory of unipolar depression. The cognitive model helps to understand how CBT is a successful treatment. The lack of social support explanation links with the idea that social isolation is a factor in schizophrenia. Choose the explanation that you feel you understand best.

A second non-biological explanation of unipolar depression is the cognitive model. This links with CBT as a therapy for unipolar depression. Depression is thought to come from a person's method of coping and their thinking processes. Distorted thinking might cause depression. The **cognitive triad** looks at a negative view of the self, the world and the future.

Table 16 Strengths and weaknesses of the cognitive model of depression

Strengths	Weaknesses
Kistner et al. (2006) found that inaccurate self-perceptions led to more depression symptoms, so links were found relating to the cognitive model	Even with evidence that negative thinking links to depression it is hard to find evidence that it causes depression
Jacobs et al. (2008) found that 8 of the 14 studies they looked at found negative self-perception linked to depression	Neurotransmitters and brain chemistry can cause depressed thoughts, or such thoughts can alter brain chemistry. It is hard to see causation

Schizophrenia: two treatments

One biological treatment is drug therapy and one psychological treatment is CBT. These treatments can suit depression as well, so you could choose them for both disorders to become more familiar with them.

Drug therapy for schizophrenia

Drug therapy picks up on the neurotransmitter explanation. If schizophrenia comes from excess dopamine then phenothiazines, for example, which block dopamine receptors so there is no excess dopamine, would be a successful therapy. Atypical or newer antipsychotic drugs have fewer side effects and act differently from typical ones. Clozapine can help with delusions and hallucinations but has serious side effects.

Table 17 Strengths and weaknesses of drug therapy for schizophrenia

Strengths	Weaknesses
Meltzer et al. (2004) found that haloperidol improves symptoms of schizophrenia and that new drugs are better than a placebo. Evidence for effectiveness is a strength of a treatment	A problem with drug therapy is that those with schizophrenia can stop taking the drugs (e.g. Guo et al., 2011, show over 30% stop)
Drug therapy rests on strong biological evidence and is supported by neurotransmitter explanations for schizophrenia. Carlsson et al. (2000) is evidence for this	Drug therapy can be seen as unacceptable and a chemical straitjacket

CBT for schizophrenia

There are cognitive symptoms in schizophrenia, such as problems with concentration, working memory and executive functioning. CBT is about thinking and learning to cope with the disorder. Drug therapy might help with some symptoms but daily living needs to be coped with and CBT can help. Specific symptoms are targeted and focused on rationally. There is belief modification and reattribution of thoughts.

Table 18 Strengths and weaknesses of CBT for schizophrenia

Strengths	Weaknesses
Hofmann et al. (2012) found there is support for CBT as a successful therapy for anxiety disorders and anger control as well as stress, and in seven reviews CBT comes out as more effective than a comparison treatment	Perhaps there are ethical problems in giving full consent for CBT and the individual has to be involved in the therapy, which might not suit everyone, depending on their level of functioning
Bentall et al. (2004a) found three of six patients reported fewer hallucinations and reduction in stress when CBT was used. It is a strength that CBT focuses beyond the schizophrenia and on the whole person	Some studies claiming effectiveness do not use controls and more randomised controlled trials are needed

Links

Individual differences link

CBT for schizophrenia would focus on individual differences and would look rationally at individual beliefs

Unipolar depression: two treatments

Questions & Answers

Clinical psychology Content Q3 covers an explanation of a biological treatment for unipolar depression.

Drug therapy for unipolar depression

Drug therapy for depression builds on neurotransmitter functioning such as serotonin functioning as an explanation for depression. Drugs can block neurotransmission at the synapse or block reuptake by the pre-synaptic neuron. Blocking reuptake leaves the neurotransmitter in the synaptic gap so it can go on passing messages between the pre- and post-synaptic neurons. Selective serotonin reuptake inhibitors (SSRIs), such as Prozac, work in this way.

Table 19 Strengths and weaknesses of drug therapy for depression

Strengths	Weaknesses
The newer atypical antidepressants have fewer side effects and are better than the old tricyclics	It can take a long time for antidepressants to start to work, which is a weakness for drugs as therapy. Perhaps they need to be prescribed alongside another therapy such as CBT
The theory about serotonin and also noradrenaline supports how drug therapy might work, and it does work, which supports the theory	Drug therapy does not give people skills for life as another therapy, such as CBT, might (Kuyken et al., 2008)

Knowledge check 9

Give two differences in CBT for schizophrenia compared with CBT for other issues and disorders.

Exam tip

There are quite a few types of antidepressant, including SSRIs and also MAOIs (monoamine oxidase inhibitors). Learn about some of these types, some specific drugs and how they work (and their side effects).

Knowledge check 10

How do SSRIs work at the synapse?

Exam tip

Effects can include withdrawal. Review what you learned about drugs and withdrawal in biological psychology.

CBT for unipolar depression

CBT is a therapy used for many disorders and is recommended by NICE guidelines in many cases as it is evidence-based. It is often used for depression as depression can come from negative thought patterns, as the cognitive model suggests. CBT helps to focus negative automatic thoughts. Features include looking at unhelpful thinking like **catastrophising** and all-or-nothing thinking.

Knowledge check 11

How is catastrophising unhelpful?

Links

Developmental psychology link

CBT can look at how early experiences have led to core beliefs about self, the world and the future and in that way can focus on someone's developmental path.

Table 20 Strengths and weaknesses of CBT for depression

Strengths	Weaknesses
Stiles et al. (2006) found that CBT was effective, though person-centred and psychodynamic therapies were effective too. Farrer et al. (2011) found internet-based CBT is effective for depression	Faulty thinking might be from the depression, not a cause of it, so CBT might help the symptoms without helping the cause (though is still helpful)
NICE guidelines support the use of CBT and it is part of IAPT (Improving Access to Psychological Therapies) and is available on the NHS, which suggests it is effective	Effectiveness comes from studies using self-report data, which might mean clients and patients support the therapist by agreeing that the therapy works, which might make data lack validity

Individual differences

The importance of individual differences has been noted in the above content section for clinical psychology. In summary, diagnosis can depend on individuals because people become distressed in different situations, and treatment such as CBT focuses on issues for each individual.

Developmental psychology

The importance of issues for our development has been noted in the above content section for clinical psychology. In summary, experiences such as social adversity and having or not having social support may link to schizophrenia, which means looking at someone's development. Treatment such as CBT looks at the effect of early experiences on later mental health and so examines someone's developmental path.

Knowledge check 12

How does the HCPC have power over a clinical psychologist?

Methods

HCPC guidelines for clinical practitioners

Standards relate to a psychologist's character, their health and their conduct, including their ethics. Clinical psychologists must attend to boundaries and power in their relationship with clients as well as confidentiality and getting informed consent.

Exam tip

It is useful to know why content is included in your course, such as why HCPC guidelines are important, as well as what the content is. By understanding issues you can give a detailed and more confident answer.

Researching mental health: methodological issues

Longitudinal studies are where one or more participants are researched over time and scores noted so that their development can be charted. As the same people are used, participant variables are controlled for.

Cross-sectional studies are where different groups are studied at one moment in time, such as people in different age groups. There can then be comparisons about development over time but not using the same people. This is quicker than using longitudinal methods and people do not drop out; however, there might be participant differences affecting results.

Cross-cultural methods involve using participants in different cultures so that they can be compared to look for similarities and differences between cultures. Universality can be studied — if a result is found in many different cultures, perhaps this means it is in our nature.

Meta-analyses involve using the findings of different studies that have used the same or a very similar research method so that the findings can be pooled. This gives a larger sample and more findings, hopefully showing reliability and generalisability.

Secondary data are where the data are already collected by other researchers when they are being used, and **primary data** are data that researchers collect themselves, first hand.

Case studies, including an example

Questions & Answers

Clinical psychology Methods Q1 looks at evaluation points about case studies and includes mention of Lavarenne et al. (2013) as an example.

Case studies are in-depth and detailed studies of one person or a small group and, focusing on individuals, they are interested in **qualitative data**, though can use **quantitative data** too. They use different methods within them, such as observation, questionnaires and researching someone's history. They tend to have validity because they focus on someone's 'real life', and they can show reliability if they use different methods. However, **generalising** from them is difficult because of the limited sample.

Lavarenne et al. (2013) is a case study looking at one session of a support group for those with psychosis to uncover the role of the group and the boundary it set for the individuals within it, who had 'fragile ego boundaries'.

Interviews, including an example

Interviews can be structured, unstructured or semi-structured and tend to gather **self-report data**. Someone asks questions directly. The questions can be completely prepared, like a questionnaire, or there can be a general schedule showing what the focus of the interview will be. Probing can help to add depth and detail and is found in an unstructured interview. Qualitative data are gathered, though there can be some quantitative data. There should be validity, though **social desirability** as well as **subjectivity** in analysing the data can bring bias.

Exam tip

Use a glossary of your own to define terms and add an example and some evaluation. Then you are ready for 'definition' questions.

Knowledge check 13

What is a main difference between longitudinal and cross-sectional designs?

Exam tip

Have an example of a study ready for each of the method issues you need to cover, such as Hankin et al. (1998) looking at depression, gender and how depression arises in young people, which is a longitudinal design.

Exam tip

Check your specification carefully when revising to make sure you prepare everything you need. In clinical psychology you need to consider the use of case studies and an example study, for example.

Knowledge check 14

What is a main difference between case studies and interviews?

Vallentine et al. (2010) used questionnaires and semi-structured interviewing and found that psycho-education for patients in a high security hospital was of benefit to them.

> **Exam tip**
>
> A way to focus on evaluation is to use two strengths and two weaknesses, though knowing more can be useful. You can use the evaluation terms from the course — reliability, validity, objectivity, subjectivity, generalisability, credibility and ethics — as that can help.

> **Exam tip**
>
> Make a list of the terms and issues you need to understand and draw up a worksheet for yourself to explain them.

Analysis of quantitative data

For your applications in psychology you need to draw on what you learned about analysis of quantitative data. You need to know about descriptive statistics (measures of central tendency, which are mean, median and mode, and measures of dispersion, which are range and standard deviation, as well as graphs and tables) and inferential statistics. For inferential statistics, recall the issues including levels of measurement, levels of significance, Type I and Type II errors, using critical values tables, understanding the calculated value and the four tests in your course. Note that these features of analysis of data are required for child and health psychology, two of the option applications, and criminological psychology, the third option, includes correlations and meta-analyses too.

> **Exam tip**
>
> Be sure you have practised actual calculations, including percentages, fractions, descriptive statistics and the four tests, as calculations will be asked for in your exams.

Analysis of qualitative data

Thematic analysis is used to analyse qualitative data and you need to know about **grounded theory** as well.

Studies

Classic study: Rosenhan (1973)

> **Questions & Answers**
>
> Clinical psychology Studies Q1 asks for two of Rosenhan's results and so gives some information about the study.

> **Exam tip**
>
> Have some results 'numbers' ready, such as that it took on average 19 days for the patients to be released and there were 12 hospitals. This will add depth to an answer.

Rosenhan's (1973) well-known study described how people went to a hospital saying they heard something like 'thud' in their heads but otherwise they were 'themselves'. They were admitted and it took time to convince the hospital they were not suffering from schizophrenia. Rosenhan also told some hospitals that some pseudo-patients would be arriving. Although this did not in fact happen, the staff 'identified' such pseudo-patients.

> **Knowledge check 15**
>
> What is a strength of Rosenhan's (1973) study?

Contemporary study: Carlsson et al. (2000)

> **Questions & Answers**
>
> Clinical psychology Studies Q2 asks for differences in the methods of Rosenhan (1973) and Carlsson et al. (2000).

Carlsson et al. (2000) focus on reviewing neurotransmitter functioning in those with schizophrenia. The focus is the dopamine hypothesis and also the glutamate hypothesis. The study mainly gives evidence for neurotransmitters being involved in schizophrenia.

> **Exam tip**
>
> You can use Carlsson et al. when discussing the neurotransmitter explanation of schizophrenia, when looking at drug treatment for schizophrenia, as an example of animal studies and neuroimaging.

Contemporary study: Williams et al. (2013)

You need one study from a choice of two in the specification for your chosen disorder 'other than' schizophrenia. Williams et al. (2013) is one of the two studies for depression; you could also choose Kroenke et al. (2008). If you are studying OCD, use one of the two studies in the specification for OCD and if you are studying anorexia nervosa, use one of those two studies.

Williams et al. (2013) used a randomised controlled trial (RCT) and two treatments, both focusing on CBT but one with cognitive-bias modification, always focusing on treatment of depression. They found 27% of patients showed clinical change in their depression after cognitive-bias modification and when CBT was also included the improvement rose to 65%. They concluded the combination was successful.

Key question

You need to know about one key question which clinical psychology concepts and research can explain. The question must be important to today's society. One key question is looked at in this book. However, you may have studied another one and might prefer to revise that one.

What are the issues surrounding mental health in the workplace?

Describing the question

Mind reports in a survey that one in five people had had a day off because of stress and one in four thought about resigning because of stress. In November 2014 the BBC suggested that more than 11 million working days were lost each year due to stress and depression. These figures suggest that workplace stress is an issue for society, both in terms of economics and in terms of happiness of individuals.

Concepts, theories and research from clinical psychology in your course

Explaining the issues surrounding mental health in the workplace

Brown et al. (1986) found that women with social support were less likely to develop depression than those with no support. Where there was no support, 44% developed depression. Kuyken et al. (2008) found that mindfulness-based cognitive therapy, which can take place in groups, was at least as successful as Prozac. This suggests employers could help by providing space and time for such treatments.

> **Exam tip**
>
> Williams et al. (2013) can be used as evidence for the effectiveness of CBT as a treatment for depression, though make the point as well that the combination with cognitive-bias modification was effective.

> **Exam tip**
>
> Williams et al. (2013) can be used as an example of randomised controlled trials using a treatment and a waiting list control group. Make notes against studies to see how you could use them frequently to enrich your answers.

> **Knowledge check 16**
>
> What is the main advantage of RCTs that make them the sought-after research method when looking at treatment effectiveness?

Clinical psychology Key question Q1 covers issues relating to mental health in the workplace.

Exam tip

It is useful to note how to describe the key question as well as how to explain it using theories and concepts you have come across in your course. Also, if you learn the theories and concepts for one (or more) key question, you are likely to be able to use them if presented with an unseen key question in your exam paper.

Practical investigation

You will have carried out a practical within clinical psychology using a content analysis. Go back over your notes to revise what you did.

Some general ideas about the practical and what to learn

You need to carry out one summative content analysis using at least two sources such as newspapers to gather data about attitudes towards mental health in those sources. The practical must be ethical. You do not have to carry out a statistical analysis but using a Chi-squared test, for example, is good practice and will show you whether your result is statistically significant. Alternatively, you could stick to qualitative data, depending on how you carry out your content analysis.

Exam tip

Turn these ideas into questions and prepare answers, as you are likely to be asked about them. For example, 'Outline the aim of your practical (2 marks) and consider two ethical issues you addressed (2 marks each)'.

Questions & Answers

Clinical psychology Practical investigation Q1a looks at categories used in the content analysis focusing on attitudes to mental disorders.

Questions & Answers

Clinical psychology Practical investigation Q1b looks at strengths and weaknesses of the practical investigation as evaluation.

Exam tip

You might be asked to plan a practical based on a short scenario. Use your understanding of methodology from your own practical to devise a different one. In clinical psychology the practical is a summative content analysis.

Issues and debates

Issues and debates are discussed in Student Guide 4, as they are part of psychological skills as well as being threaded through the topic areas in your course.

Questions & Answers

Clinical psychology Issues and debates Q1 looks at clinical psychology as an example of psychology as science, and includes information about Popper and science.

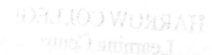

Summary

- Diagnosis and using classification systems are important in clinical psychology, as are issues of reliability and validity.
- Schizophrenia and one other disorder has to be covered. Coverage should include symptoms and features, two explanations and two treatments for each disorder (with one additional explanation for schizophrenia).
- Methods include longitudinal, cross-sectional, cross-cultural, meta-analysis and primary/ secondary data — a group not covered up to now in your course.
- HCPC guidelines for clinical psychology are required to add to what you know about ethics.
- Case studies and an example case study, and interviews and an example interview, are required.
- As covered in Year 1, a review of descriptive and inferential statistics is included in clinical psychology, as is thematic analysis to cover analysis of qualitative data. Grounded theory to analyse qualitative data is added.
- Rosenhan (1973) is the classic study and Carlsson et al. (2000) is the contemporary study on schizophrenia. You then choose one study out of two in the specification for your chosen 'other' disorder.
- A key question is required as in other topics, as is a practical investigation, this time a content analysis.

■Criminological psychology

This section looks at criminological psychology (an option application). Sections on child psychology and health psychology follow. You will have studied one of these three applications, so focus on the one you have studied. Clinical psychology is worth 54 of the 90 marks in Paper 3 and has been given more focus in this guide.

Table 21 Summary of criminological psychology in your course

Content
Explanations of crime and antisocial behaviour, including biological explanations: brain injury, amygdala and aggression, XYY syndrome, personality. Social explanations, including labelling and self-fulfilling prophecy. Gender differences in explanations of crime and anti-social behaviour. Understanding the offender by looking at cognitive and ethical interviewing as well as case formulation. A fourth section considers one cognitive–behavioural treatment and one biological treatment for offenders. Two other areas are looked at: factors influencing eyewitness testimony and factors influencing juror decision-making.
As in other topic areas, individual differences and developmental psychology need to be linked into the content studied.

Methodology
Laboratory and field experiments used to look at eyewitness issues, and case studies. The four sampling techniques from social psychology, as well as evaluation issues in the course: reliability, validity, objectivity, credibility, and ethics. Data analysis as in clinical psychology, including correlation and meta-analysis as well. Also ethical guidelines, including the BPS guidelines already covered in social psychology and HCPC guidelines for forensic psychologists.

Two studies in detail
Loftus and Palmer (1974) and Valentine and Mesout (2009) are described and evaluated. You may have studied Bradbury and Williams (2013) or Howells et al. (2005) instead.

Key question
'Is eyewitness testimony too unreliable to trust?' is chosen as the key question here, but you may have looked at one or more different key questions.

Practical
You will have carried out at least one practical in criminological psychology and you should use your own investigation, because you will have 'learned by doing'. Some ideas about the practical are suggested in this guide.

> **Exam tip**
>
> Use this table to draw up a checklist of what you need to cover in your revision. Annotate it to show what you feel you know (green tick), what just needs some brief revision (amber circle) and which areas you need to focus on (red cross).

> **Knowledge check 17**
>
> List three areas you need to cover in criminological psychology that you have covered in your course already.

Questions & Answers

Option applications Overview Q1 asks about one feature of criminological psychology.

> **Exam tip**
>
> Be ready for questions that ask you about criminological psychology in general, such as it being about the definition and causes of crime and antisocial behaviour and identification and treatment of offenders.

Explanations of crime and antisocial behaviour

Crime is an action or not doing something that is an offence and against the law. **Antisocial behaviour** refers to behaviour that goes against social norms and affects people's lives negatively but might not be against the law.

Biological explanations

Brain injury

You looked at brain damage when considering people like Henry Molaison, who suffered damage which affected his memory. Brain injury can lead to aggressive behaviour in some people. Brain injury to the frontal lobes can affect executive functioning, which includes problem solving and control over impulsivity.

The amygdala and aggression

In biological psychology you looked at brain structures and aggression, probably including the amygdala, so recall that information. Charles Whitman was responsible for killing a number of people and was thought to have had a brain tumour affecting his amygdala, although some doubt was shed on this explanation for his behaviour. A smaller amygdala can link with violence and aggression (Pardini et al., 2013).

XYY syndrome

XYY refers to a male with an additional Y chromosome at birth, so having 47 chromosomes. People with 47, XYY tend to be taller and can have severe acne. Such males can have reduced intelligence and learning difficulties, though there is a lot of normal functioning and there are individual differences.

Links

Developmental psychology link

XYY syndrome affects someone's biological development and also their experiences, including how they are treated, so it affects their overall development.

Links

Individual differences link

Those with XYY syndrome are not all the same, though being taller seems a common identifiable trait. Some have lower intelligence, but not all.

Jacobs et al. (1965) suggested XYY led people to be more aggressive and it has been suggested that there are more people with XYY in the criminal population than would be expected given the frequency in the general population.

Personality

Temperament refers to a part of our personality that we seem to be born with. Personality traits are tendencies to act in certain ways. Eysenck thought we have

Exam tip

Be ready to use material from one part of your course and apply it to another. For example, the strengths and weaknesses you learned about regarding scanning can be used to evaluate brain injury as an explanation of crime and antisocial behaviour, such as that scanning has reliability.

Knowledge check 18

Give one weakness of the amygdala explanation of crime and antisocial behaviour.

dimensions to our personality. Extraversion–introversion is one dimension, neuroticism–stability is another and there is also a psychoticism dimension. Criminal behaviour tends to link to extraversion, neuroticism and psychoticism.

Links

Individual differences link

Each person's personality will be unique to them.

Social explanations

Labelling

People can be labelled, leading to stereotyping, which affects how people behave. We react to our labels. **Labelling** tends to occur when a majority sees a minority as inferior and it tends to be negative for the person being labelled. A label can be a stigma, which affects our self-concept and self-identity.

Self-fulfilling prophecy

Labels can be self-fulfilling. If someone is called aggressive, their aggressive behaviour may be noticed by others and commented upon, which affects how the person reacts, and their reaction could well be aggressive. The **self-fulfilling prophecy** suggests that someone is given an untrue label which affects their self-esteem and the person then behaves according to their label, thus it becomes self-fulfilling.

Links

Developmental psychology link

Being affected by a self-fulfilling prophecy means being affected by one's development.

Focus on gender differences

There are gender differences in explanations for criminality, and some are suggested here. Brain injury shows similar effects in males and females, although there are gender differences in the actual injuries incurred. Gender differences in neurobiology can relate to amygdala functioning, for example Zahn-Waxler (2000, cited in Shirtcliff et al., 2009) found girls show more empathy than boys. XYY applies only to males, so if it had linked to antisocial behaviour and crime that would explain a focus on males and aggression. However, the link between XYY and crime is not upheld by evidence in general.

Exam tip

Check your specification carefully to make sure you cover everything. The comment about considering gender differences in explanations of crime and antisocial behaviour is clear but easily overlooked as it is in the heading rather than being a separate point.

Exam tip

As personality is a biological explanation of crime and antisocial behaviour, be ready to show how it comes from our biological make-up, for example links to speed of arousal.

Knowledge check 19

Compare one biological with one social explanation for crime and antisocial behaviour.

Exam tip

Use terms such as 'self-concept' and 'self-fulfilling prophecy' in your answers to show your understanding. Putting together your own glossary can help. You could use index cards with a term on one side and its definition on the other and then use the cards to test yourself.

Understanding the offender, offence analysis and case formulation

Cognitive interview

A **cognitive interview** is a way of getting as much recall as possible from a witness. Focus is on mentally reinstating the environment and people, giving all the details whether they are thought to be important or not, giving the description in a different order and starting from different places and also giving the story by imagining the viewpoint of different people that were there.

Ethical interview

There are ethical standards for interviewing relating to crime, including every human being having worth and needing to be treated with dignity and interviews being non-judgemental and open with no coercion or gain by the interviewer. PEACE involves **p**lanning and preparing, **e**ngaging and explaining, getting the **a**ccount that is required, bringing **c**losure at the end of the interview and then **e**valuating the interview.

Psychological formulation

Forensic psychologists are involved in assessing offenders, putting together a formulation and then carrying out an intervention. The **case formulation** takes the information from the assessment and brings in theory to put together a treatment plan.

Links

Developmental psychology link

An assessment, on which a formulation rests, can include influences on the individual's development, for example biological aspects like learning difficulties or environmental aspects such as abuse or not having good role models.

Links

Individual differences link

A formulation is personal and relates just to one individual. You will look at the case study as a research method in criminological psychology. Case studies focus on individuals and often at the function of offending behaviour for that individual.

Two treatments for offenders

You need to know two treatments, one cognitive–behavioural and one biological. For both treatments you need a study as well.

One cognitive–behavioural treatment: anger management

Anger management is chosen here. A group has a check-in at the start, rules about listening to one another, discussions of what makes each person angry and positive thoughts about each person's progress, what they enjoy and something positive about

> **Exam tip**
>
> For ideas like cognitive interviewing, make sure you have enough information about the effectiveness or not of the technique. When you are learning about something practical, such as interviewing techniques, effectiveness is important.

> **Exam tip**
>
> The section of criminological psychology that is about understanding the offender includes the use of formulation to understand the function of the offending behaviour for the individual. The question is how behaving in that way works for that individual. Note this aspect of your course.

someone they dislike. The cognitive–behavioural element is that their angry thinking (cognitive) and responses (behaviour) are challenged and hopefully replaced.

One study of anger management effectiveness

Howells et al. (2005) is chosen because it is a contemporary study in your course. The researchers found that the control group reduced their anger, as did the treatment group, so the treatment did not work in that the treatment group did not do better. They found that readiness for the treatment and being motivated to do the treatment correlated with better outcomes. Howells et al. thought the control group became interested as all the assessment they had seemed to help them to show reduced measures of anger — so in a way the treatment did work, as the control group had the same reduction as the treatment group.

Links

Developmental psychology link

If someone's past experiences trigger anger, this suggests developmental issues.

One biological treatment: hormone treatment

Hormone treatment focuses on sex offenders and the use of drugs to normalise sexual drives. Anti-androgens reduce sexual drives and deviant fantasies. There are also other drugs that are not anti-androgens, such as medroxyprogesterone acetate (MPA).

One study of hormone treatment effectiveness

Maletsky et al. (2006) found that anti-androgens led to lower rates of sexual recidivism and decreased sexual arousal compared with not having the treatment. They looked at using MPA (trade name depo-Provera). It was found that in those receiving MPA new offences and any violation of parole were much reduced.

Links

Developmental psychology link

If hormone treatment affects someone's (criminal) behaviour then perhaps hormones are a cause of such behaviour, which relates to their development.

Factors influencing eyewitness testimony

Loftus and Palmer (1974), the classic study in this topic, found that the verb in a question affected estimate of speed. The question came after the event, so was **post-event information**, which is a factor you need to focus on.

Exam tip

Unreliability of eyewitness testimony is the key question here. It involves experiments, so fits with methods; it involves the classic and contemporary study chosen here; and it can be the focus of the practical investigation. You can use the material in different sections of this application.

Exam tip

When you are asked to cover a study, such as a study of effectiveness for each of the two treatments for offenders in criminological psychology, cover enough of the study to give the aims, methods, results, conclusions and evaluation points as you would for other studies.

Exam tip

If a biological treatment helps in dealing with offending behaviour, as MPA helped sexual offenders, then that can be used as evidence that such offences are biological in nature.

Exam tip

If you use Maletsky et al. (2006), note that they used Chi-squared tests and talk about the findings being significant at $p < 0.0001$, for example. You can use studies as examples when you discuss methodological issues.

Knowledge check 20

What does it mean to say a result of a study is significant at $p < 0.0001$? Would this level of significance link more to a Type II or a Type I error?

Post-event information

Yuille and Cutshall (1986) found good recall by eyewitnesses of a real event after 4 or 5 months had elapsed, so **post-event information** might not affect memory of a real event as much as it seems from experiments. Yuille and Cutshall (1986) planted information such as there being a yellow quarter panel (in fact it was blue), and witnesses were not misled. However, experiments such as Loftus et al. (1978) show that post-event information does affect recall; in their experiment those asked about a yield sign recalled one even though what was there was a stop sign.

> **Exam tip**
>
> In cognitive psychology you looked at reconstructive memory and how we might use schemas to guide our thinking, coming from our experiences. Post-event information can be incorporated into a memory, which then becomes reconstructed. Memory is not like a tape-recording that cannot be altered. You can use your understanding of such theories to help discussion.

Weapon focus

The **weapon focus** effect is where a weapon in a scene is more likely to be focused on and so other information is not well recalled.

Factors influencing jury decision-making

Jury decision-making is supposed to focus on facts in a crime. However, jurors have other information to draw on that might bias their decisions.

Characteristics of the defendant

- Bradbury and Williams (2013), a contemporary study in this application, shows how the race of the majority of the jury, if white or Hispanic, can influence judgement of a black defendant. Other studies, however, have not found that race is a factor affecting juror decision-making.
- The gender of the defendant can be a factor. Ahola et al. (2009), in **mock jury trials**, found female defendants tended to have shorter sentences than males in certain crimes, including homicide. However, as with race, studies have found no difference with regard to defendant gender.
- Another characteristic is physical attractiveness. Sigall and Ostrove (1975) found that a crime related to attractiveness, like swindling someone, meant that an attractive defendant had a harsher sentence whereas as a crime like burglary, not related to attractiveness, meant a more lenient sentence for an attractive defendant.
- Gunnell and Ceci (2010) looked at the processing preferences of jurors. They found that experientially processing people (processing emotionally) were harsher with less attractive defendants than people who processed rationally. In other words, it was not just the attractiveness of the defendant but also the processing preference of the juror.

> **Exam tip**
>
> When discussing issues such as the weapon focus effect and the effect of post-event information (and, later, factors influencing juror decision-making), use evidence in the form of studies and have ready some figures regarding their results, as well as evaluation points. This adds depth to a discussion.

> **Knowledge check 21**
>
> When it is claimed that information after an event and a weapon being present in an event are both likely to affect eyewitness recall, how is this evidence for unreliability of eyewitness testimony?

> **Exam tip**
>
> In social psychology you learned about in-group favouritism and out-group hostility, leading to prejudice. If the juror identifies with the defendant (or the victim), for example by gender or race or other characteristic, there might be in-group favouritism. Use your understanding of theory in discussion where it 'fits'.

Pre-trial publicity

Jurors can also be affected by what they read and hear about a trial before they are part of the jury. Steblay et al. (1999) found that trials exposed to negative **pre-trial publicity** tended to lead to a guilty verdict more than was the case in trials that were either not exposed to such publicity or were exposed to only limited pre-trial publicity.

Individual differences

The importance of individual differences has been noted in the above content section for criminological psychology. In summary, there are individual differences in people with XYY syndrome, and people's personality is unique to them. A formulation is personal, relating to someone's individual differences. When jurors process information they do so as individuals and this can affect how they judge a defendant.

Developmental psychology

The importance of issues for our development has been noted in the above content section for criminological psychology. In summary, XYY syndrome will affect someone's development. An assessment and formulation will involve past experiences and developmental issues for the individual. Anger can be attributed to past experiences and someone's development can be affected by a self-fulfilling prophecy. Hormones can link to behaviour including criminal behaviour, which can be a developmental issue.

Methods

Lab and field experiments and eyewitness testimony

Features of experiments are briefly explained in the table.

Table 22 Features of experiments as a research method

Feature	Brief explanation
Manipulated **independent variable (IV)**	A research question gives a specific focus arising from theory and variables are **operationalised** to make them measurable and able to be manipulated — such as the verb in a question ('smashed' versus 'hit') or the arousal level of someone who has seen a 'scary person'. What is manipulated to see its effect is the independent variable
Measured dependent variable	The result of manipulating the independent variable is the **dependent variable (DV)** and this is what is measured. An example might be the estimated speed of the car or whether the 'scary person' is identified or not
Control over **extraneous variables**	Apart from the IV and the DV, all other variables must be controlled for, including **participant variables** and **situational variables**. These might be gender or age (participant) or noise in the environment (situational)
No **confounding variables**	If all other variables are controlled for, there are no confounding variables and cause-and-effect conclusions are drawn
An experimental hypothesis can be statistically tested	The experimental **hypothesis** is accepted if the results are statistically significant and the theory supported and/or more testing is done

Field experiments are the same as **laboratory experiments** in many of their features. However, they are carried out in the natural setting and situation, not in the artificial controlled laboratory, so there is more validity. On the other hand, there is less ability to control what is going on around the situation, which means they can lack reliability.

Exam tip

When discussing lab and field experiments in criminological psychology, you are likely to be asked to focus on eyewitness testimony. Be sure to stick to discussing that area rather than straying into another area such as mock jury trials, unless you are asked to do so.

Case studies

The **case study** research method was briefly outlined on page 19. Use case studies in criminological psychology as examples, such as Arsuffi (2010), who looked at one person, to consider the assessment, formulation and treatment involved.

Sampling techniques

Random, **stratified**, **opportunity** and **volunteer** sampling are the four chosen for your course and you covered them in social psychology. Random is the best when it comes to generalising, as people are randomly allocated into conditions and so there is not likely to be bias.

Exam tip

In social psychology you covered the four sampling techniques including their strengths and weaknesses so use that material in criminological psychology as well. Look for studies you have covered that use these types of sampling, to add evidence to any discussion.

Evaluation issues

In criminological psychology you are asked to consider issues of reliability, validity, objectivity, credibility and ethics in research. You will have been covering such issues in your study of the content and other material in this application.

- For example, there is **reliability** in laboratory experiments because of their careful controls which make them replicable. Loftus and Palmer's (1974) study can be replicated.
- However, field experiments might have more **validity** because they are not in an unnatural setting for the participants, such as Yarmey (2004), who used people who were in the area. Yarmey (2004) in this way used opportunity sampling.
- **Objectivity** relates more to laboratory experiments than case studies because there does not have to be any interpretation of results — the dependent variable is measurable objectively. Case studies might gather qualitative data and there can be interpretation, such as in deciding which data to record.

Exam tip

You learned about experiments, including lab and field experiments, in cognitive psychology. Draw on that knowledge.

Knowledge check 22

What is the difference between extraneous and confounding variables?

Exam tip

You have covered information about case studies in cognitive psychology such as the case of Henry Molaison. Draw up a table comparing strengths and weaknesses of case studies and experiments when researching in criminological psychology, drawing on what you already know as well.

Knowledge check 23

For one of the four sampling techniques, explain how one study within criminological psychology uses the sampling technique.

- **Credibility** goes with using a scientific method like an experiment because cause-and-effect conclusions can be demonstrated, as in Loftus's experimental work. However, case studies can show credibility (perhaps a different type of credibility) in that they are about real-life issues.
- **Ethics** are referred to below.

Ethical guidelines

BPS Code of Ethics and Conduct (2009) and risk management

Respect, responsibility, integrity and competence are the four ethical principles in the BPS code. Within those are specifics such as a researcher getting informed consent and giving right to withdraw throughout a study, as well as ensuring there is confidentiality and privacy and no harm is done to a participant. Risk management is also important; you can review your notes about risk management from when you covered that area in social psychology.

> **Exam tip**
>
> For each of the ethical principles, aim to have an example from your course, in this case from criminological psychology. For example, Valentine and Mesout's (2009) participants were told they could withdraw at any time and did not have to give a reason.

HCPC principles for carrying out formulation and intervention

Health and Care Professions Council (HCPC) standards of proficiency are about being able to practise safely and effectively within legal and ethical boundaries of the profession. Focus is on competence and integrity, and also the important principle of doing no harm.

> **Exam tip**
>
> You can access the HCPC standards of proficiency using the internet. Explore a little as there is a lot in the document. See where there is special mention of forensic psychology. You can use the document for clinical psychology as well, where HCPC guidelines are also mentioned.

Analysis of data

You need to cover the issues around analysis of quantitative data, as explained in clinical psychology (page 20), and to add correlation and meta-analysis to that list. You also need to cover analysis of qualitative data, focusing on thematic analysis and grounded theory, as in clinical psychology.

> **Questions & Answers**
>
> Option applications Method Q1 is a method question focusing on hypotheses and inferential testing.

> **Exam tip**
>
> Check your understanding of the evaluation issues listed in this section. An example of each can be helpful, ready for discussion in an exam question.

> **Knowledge check 24**
>
> Give three reasons why ethics are so important when researching in criminological psychology and three reasons why ethics are important for a practising psychologist, like a forensic psychologist.

> **Exam tip**
>
> HCPC is a common abbreviation. In an exam answer, spell out the full title of anything abbreviated. Put the shortened term afterwards in brackets and then use the shortened term. Only use this strategy for abbreviations that are common.

Studies

Classic study: Loftus and Palmer (1974)

Loftus and Palmer's (1974) study is very useful for the key question about the unreliability of eyewitness testimony, as a laboratory experiment looking at eyewitness testimony and as a study looking at post-event information affecting eyewitness testimony. In the study, student participants were shown a film of a car accident and then asked questions about it. The researchers found that using the verb 'smashed' when asking for estimate of speed gave a higher estimate than using 'hit'.

Contemporary study: Valentine and Mesout (2009)

You have three contemporary studies to choose from. They are Valentine and Mesout (2009), Bradbury and Williams (2013) and Howells et al. (2005). Valentine and Mesout (2009) is summarised below. It suits the key question that is used here. It is also a field study and has useful method features, as well as focusing on eyewitness identification, and so is relevant in the content section too. However, if you have studied one of the other two studies, you might prefer to revise your own chosen study. Your textbook will give you more detail.

Valentine and Mesout (2009) used people who were visiting the London Dungeon and set up a 'scary person' to be in part of the dungeon (the labyrinth), on the tour. After the tour the participants were questioned about the 'scary person', including being asked to identify the person. The participants were also rated for their anxiety level. The researchers found that women reported higher state anxiety in the labyrinth than men and that the higher someone's anxiety the less accurately they reported the appearance of the 'scary person'.

Key question

You need to know about one key question which criminological psychology concepts and research can explain. The question must be important to today's society. One key question is looked at in this book. However, you may have studied another one and might prefer to revise that one.

Is eyewitness testimony too unreliable to trust?

Describing the question

Eyewitnesses are an important part of the court system today and are relied upon. For example, a juror is supposed to take evidence into account and will see witness testimony as evidence, perhaps precisely because the witness has a role in the court proceedings and that gives them credence. Kirk Bloodworth was convicted of rape and murder in 1984 and was released after 9 years when DNA testing showed him to be innocent.

Concepts, theories and research from criminological psychology in your course

Explaining whether eyewitness testimony is too unreliable to trust

You have looked at post-event information and weapon focus and seen that eyewitness memory is affected by factors in the person or in the surroundings biasing eyewitness testimony. Yuille and Cutshall (1986) shows witness testimony to be reliable in a real-life case, so perhaps the unreliability is found only in experiments, though real-life examples like Kirk Bloodworth suggest otherwise.

> **Exam tip**
>
> Be sure to have plenty of theory (perhaps reconstructive theory), concepts (perhaps weapon focus) and research (such as Loftus and Palmer, 1974, and other studies) to discuss in your explanation of your key question. You might be asked for two concepts, for example, so be ready to use what you have learned.

Practical investigation

You will have carried out a practical within criminological psychology if you chose this option, using an experiment, a questionnaire or an interview. Go back over your notes to revise what you did.

> **Questions & Answers**
>
> Option applications Practical investigation Q1 asks about 'your' practical investigation and how you could improve it.

Some general ideas about the practical and what to learn

For the practical investigation in criminological psychology, you need to carry out a questionnaire, interview or experiment. You need to include a research question/hypothesis, research method, sampling, ethical considerations, data collection tools, data analysis, results and discussion, as well as quantitative data and statistical analysis of the data. You should also look at the strengths and weaknesses of the practical and at possible improvements.

> **Exam tip**
>
> It is important to describe the question itself, such as why it poses a problem for society or the individual. Here people can be wrongly imprisoned if eyewitness testimony is unreliable and the guilty can go free, which can lead to more victims. Unreliability in eyewitness testimony has important consequences.

> **Knowledge check 26**
>
> Give two reasons why you would not trust eyewitness testimony if you were a judge.

> **Exam tip**
>
> Practise using these ideas as questions and prepare answers. For example, give the research question and outline what data collection tools were used, as well as results and a discussion.

Issues and debates

Issues and debates are discussed in Student Guide 4, as they are part of psychological skills as well as being threaded through the topic areas in your course.

Summary: criminological psychology

- Biological and social explanations of crime and antisocial behaviour are required.
- Understanding the offender, including cognitive and ethical interviewing, as well as case formulation, is needed.
- There is focus on one biological and one non-biological treatment for offenders.
- Factors influencing eyewitness memory and factors influencing juror decision-making are required.
- Methods include lab and field experiments and case studies, as well as the four sampling techniques in your course and evaluation issues: reliability, validity, objectivity, credibility and ethics.
- Methods include analysis of qualitative and quantitative data, as in clinical psychology, but with the addition of meta-analysis and correlation.

- Ethics are required, including the BPS *Code of Ethics and Conduct* (2009) and risk management, and also the HCPC principles for psychologists carrying out formulation and intervention.
- Loftus and Palmer (1974) is the classic study; Valentine and Mesout (2009) is a contemporary study, but you can use Bradbury and Williams (2013) or Howells et al. (2005) instead.
- As with other topics, one key question for society is wanted and this is a free choice.
- You need to carry out a questionnaire, interview or experiment in an area related to criminological psychology for your course. This is the practical investigation.

■ Child psychology

This section looks at child psychology (an option application). Sections on criminological psychology and health psychology are found elsewhere in this guide. You will have studied one of these three applications, so focus on the one you have studied. Clinical psychology is worth 54 of the 90 marks in Paper 3 and has been given more focus in this guide.

Table 23 Summary of child psychology in your course

Content
Bowlby's and Ainsworth's work on attachment, as well as research into deprivation and the reduction of negative effects, and research into privation and whether negative effects can be reversed. Coverage of the Strange Situation is included within this material. Research into day care, including pros and cons of day care for the child and high quality and poor quality day care. Cross-cultural research into attachment types and nature–nurture issues as required in the content and also in the methods section. Finally, autism, including features, one biological and one other explanation, and therapies for helping children with autism.
As in other topic areas, individual differences and developmental psychology need to be linked into the content studied.
Methodology
Focus is on observations, questionnaires and interviews as research methods, bringing in aspects covered in Year 1 (such as participant, non-participant, overt and covert types of observation). Cross-cultural research and universality issues, and meta-analysis, being the method used in the classic study. Ethics of researching with children are covered, as well as analysis of quantitative data including descriptive and inferential statistics, and analysis of qualitative data.
Two studies in detail
The classic van Ijzendoorn and Kroonenberg (1988) and the contemporary study Cassibba et al. (2013) are described and evaluated. You may have chosen Gagnon-Oosterwaal et al. (2012) or Li et al. (2013) instead as your contemporary study.
Key question
'What issues should parents take into account when deciding about day care for their child?' is chosen as the key question here, but you may have looked at one or more different key questions.
Practical
You will have carried out at least one practical in child psychology and you should use your own investigation, because you will have 'learned by doing'. Some ideas about the practical are suggested in this guide.

> ### Exam tip
> Use this table to draw up a checklist of what you need to cover in your revision. Annotate it to show what you feel you know (green tick), what just needs some brief revision (amber circle) and which areas you cannot remember much about (red cross).

> ### Exam tip
> Be ready for questions that ask you about child psychology in general, as well as specific material that you cover in your course.

Attachment, deprivation and privation

Questions & Answers

Option applications Content Q1 asks about definitions of attachment and privation.

> ### Knowledge check 27
> Give a short definition of child psychology.

Bowlby's work on attachment

Bowlby's **maternal deprivation hypothesis** suggests that without an **attachment** figure a child is deprived and this will affect their later development. Bowlby's 44 Juvenile Thieves study showed that being deprived of a mother or caregiver in early life can lead to affectionless psychopathy. Our early attachment experiences give us an **internal working model** for later relationships.

Bowlby looked at deprivation. For more about his ideas, see below under the headings 'Research into deprivation' and 'How negative effects can be reduced'.

Links

Developmental psychology link

Maternal deprivation and the internal working model, as well as the focus on loss and how later experiences are affected by early ones, all clearly relate to development.

Ainsworth's work on attachment

Ainsworth looked at attachment types and found three — secure, ambivalent insecure and avoidant insecure attachments. A fourth type, disorganised insecure attachment, was added later.

Types of attachment

Ainsworth's observations in Uganda and Baltimore (in the USA) showed her that the infant–mother interaction and bond was similar in the different cultures and that the three main types of attachment were present in both. In Uganda she observed **sensitive mothering** led to securely attached infants (the largest 'type'). The mother is a **safe base** for the child to explore from, and the child shows **separation anxiety**, a sign of being securely attached.

- **Secure attachment** (Type B) means the child is distressed when the mother leaves and goes to the mother for comfort on her return.
- **Ambivalent insecure** (Type C, also called **anxious resistant**) means the child is very distressed when the mother leaves, goes for comfort on her return and then rejects the comfort.
- **Avoidant insecure** (Type A, also called **anxious avoidant**) means the child is not distressed when the mother leaves and tends to avoid her when she returns.
- **Disorganised insecure/disoriented** means the child approaches the mother on her return and also avoids her. The child can dissociate from the situation and detach from it, so the attachment is 'disorganised'.

Strange Situation procedure

The **Strange Situation procedure** is a structured observation procedure originally carried out by Ainsworth. It involves a mother and infant interacting with a stranger, with the mother and stranger leaving and arriving into the room where the infant is. The reunions between the mother and infant are the focus of the observation. The infant's behaviour is classified into a 'type', as described by Ainsworth and her team.

Exam tip

Bowlby worked within psychodynamic principles. As with others working in that field, he felt that it was 'loss' that characterised problems like depression and that our early experiences affect later relationships (and, therefore, problems). Draw on what you learned about psychodynamic principles in biological psychology.

Exam tip

In your exam you may be given stimulus material to answer questions about. In child psychology such material might describe a situation and ask you to discuss the attachment type or types of a child or children in the source. Be ready to apply understanding of attachment types to 'real-life' situations.

Knowledge check 28

Name three features/terms relating to the child being securely attached.

Links

Developmental psychology link

An attachment is a bond between infant and caregiver and it seems that parenting style can affect attachment type, which affects later development.

Research into deprivation

Deprivation is when an infant has a broken attachment for a short time, such as when there is separation (e.g. day care) or for a long time (e.g. through divorce). **Privation** is when an infant does not form an attachment at all.

Short-term and long-term effects

The Robertsons looked at short-term deprivation, such as when a child or mother was in hospital, and they found a young child suffered a great deal when deprived of their attachment figure. Introducing the child to a carer and putting careful fostering in place alleviated the distress somewhat. There are three stages when a child's attachment breaks: **protest**, **despair** and **detachment**.

The long-term effect of deprivation from separation was shown by Bowlby in his 44 Juvenile Thieves study to be affectionless psychopathy. Spitz found depression in children experiencing long-term deprivation, which he called 'hospitalism'. Goldfarb found that early adoption or fostering helped a child, as they could form new attachments, but if left too long this led to a child being emotionally less secure and intellectually behind others. Olsavsky et al. (2013) suggested a link between maternal deprivation and reduced amygdala discrimination, where deprivation might lead a child to show friendliness to 'anyone'. fMRI scanning was used to look at amygdala response.

How negative effects can be reduced

Avoiding separation can reduce the negative effects of deprivation but, if this is impossible, reducing the length of separation can help. In the short term, as the Robertsons found, having a replacement attachment figure can be of benefit. In the longer term, stimulation and support can help, including, in care, a better adult-to-child ratio and more one-to-one attention. Any intervention should be as early as possible. With more good quality care and more stimulation, early effects of deprivation can be reduced — depending on the age of the child and how long the deprivation has lasted.

Links

Developmental psychology link

Deprivation affects the long-term development of a child, though its effects can be reduced by good quality care and stimulation.

Exam tip

Understanding the Strange Situation procedure is important because it is part of the method in this application and is also used in the classic study. It is also used in the contemporary study chosen here for this application. Both studies are meta-analyses involving studies that used the Strange Situation procedure.

Exam tip

Your course asks for 'research into deprivation' so you need to mention studies as well as give detail about concepts.

Exam tip

Note that you need to know about research into the short- and long-term effects of deprivation and also how negative effects can be reduced. Draw up a table with relevant research and a brief account of what was found and how you can use the findings to answer questions in this area.

Links

Individual differences link

It is interesting that not much is said in Bowlby's and Ainsworth's research about individual differences such as the temperament of the child, as that, and the individual parenting style, have been shown to affect attachments. Thomas and Chess look at child temperament and consider there are 'difficult' and 'easy' children, as well as 'fearful' ones. Perhaps temperament is innate and affects infant–caregiver attachment patterns.

Research into privation

Curtiss (1977) studied Genie, a young girl who had been severely privated and was found at the age of about 13 years. She developed some language and, with care, made progress. However, the effects of her early privation were not reversed.

Jarmila Koluchová (1972) studied twins in Czechoslovakia who, it is thought, did have some normal development but then at a very young age were institutionalised. When their father remarried he took them back into the family home, where they were severely privated. When they were found at the age of seven they were very much 'behind' for their age in terms of IQ, for example. However, unlike Genie, they made good progress and as far as we know went on to lead 'normal' lives. The effects of their early privation were reversed.

Eigsti et al. (2011) studied children who had been internationally adopted (adopted by a family from a different country) and they found there were long-term issues in language and cognitive abilities, depending on factors such as the age at which the children were adopted. This suggests some effect from early privation and that perhaps some effects cannot be reversed.

Whether negative effects can be reversed

Koluchová (1972) reported that the twins she studied were cared for intensively after they were found, with a lot of stimulation, and it was thought that this intensive caring was what led to them 'catching up' on their development. Curtiss' study of Genie suggested the negative effects could not be reversed and Eigsti et al. also suggest there are language and cognitive issues that are not reversible. However, the twins had one another and also some care at the start of their lives compared with Genie, who seemed not to have any attachment in her life. Eigsti et al. also suggest that early adoption and good quality care can reverse adverse effects for internationally adopted children.

Knowledge check 29

In discussing whether the effects of privation or deprivation can be reduced or reversed, and considering how this might be done, we see there are similarities in how the effects of poor early attachments can be overcome. What are two main ways that seem to be suggested to overcome both privation and deprivation effects?

Exam tip

You can take day care as a form of separation. Ideas about reducing any negative effects of a child being in day care are given on page 40. These areas — deprivation, privation, attachment types and day care — are not as separate as they might seem.

Exam tip

When asked to consider research, such as being asked for research into privation and whether negative effects can be reversed, be sure to have studies ready. You could be asked to evaluate the research, for example, which means evaluating the methods used.

Exam tip

There is evidence showing that negative effects of privation can be reversed and evidence showing that this does not happen. Be ready to offer evidence for both sides of the argument.

Research into day care

Day care can be seen as a form of separation from a caregiver, which is a form of deprivation, though short-term separation might not affect a child if there is good quality replacement care, as the Robertsons found. There are clear rules for day care providers, concerning aspects such as washing facilities, number of staff, window and floor space, and how many children are in the room depending on the size of the space.

Advantages and disadvantages for the child

Day care can have advantages for one child and disadvantages for another child. Good quality day care is beneficial because it offers stimulation and different experiences from what a child encounters at home. There are negatives with day care, however, such as if the care is of poor quality and there is no good stimulation. Also, the age of the child can affect whether or not day care is good. Being under one year old and spending too long in day care (more than 20 hours a week) can be detrimental, for example.

There are pros and cons with day care, and the type of day care makes a difference. One of the findings about nursery day care is that it can lead to improvements in cognitive and language development. However, it can also lead to more behavioural problems — children spending longer in day care early in their lives are more likely to have later behavioural problems. The quality of day care is also important, with low quality care being particularly bad for children with less sensitive mothers. High quality day care tends to give better language and cognitive development and results in more co-operative children. Also, where each staff member has fewer children to look after, this gives more positive care.

What makes good and poor quality day care

Good quality care is characterised by: fewer children per adult; smaller groups; staff with a high level of education; staff showing a positive, cheerful attitude; staff asking questions and encouraging children to speak; hugging and having positive physical contact with the child; and praising or encouraging. Poor quality day care would be characterised by the opposite of these ideas, such as one member of staff being responsible for quite a high number of children (though this is regulated), staff not interacting with the children as much, and less praising taking place.

Links

Developmental psychology link

When day care is said to be advantageous or disadvantageous for a child this means how it affects their development.

Individual differences link

Belsky and Pluess (2011) found that low quality day care in particular affected a child with a 'difficult' temperament, so individual differences are important when considering the pros and cons of day care for a child.

> **Exam tip**
>
> What issues a parent should take into account when choosing day care for their child is the key question for society chosen in this application. You can use the information about the pros and cons of day care when discussing the key question.

> **Knowledge check 30**
>
> What three issues around day care might a parent take into account when choosing day care for their child?

> **Exam tip**
>
> In this section, as in other sections in child psychology, you are asked to look at research into day care (including advantages and disadvantages, as well as what makes good and poor quality day care for a child). This means bringing in evidence from studies, so be sure to do that.

Cross-cultural research into attachment types and nature–nurture issues

Cross-cultural studies looking at attachment types have used the Strange Situation procedure (see page 37). Jin et al. (2012) found 78% securely attached, 1% anxious avoidant and 21% anxious resistant. Ainsworth's Baltimore findings generally were about 70% securely attached, 15% anxious avoidant and 15% anxious resistant. You can see similarities in the findings (as well as differences). These sorts of findings were what led to it being held that attachment types are universals. **Universals** refer to characteristics that are found in all cultures and, therefore, thought to be down to human nature and not to nurture.

Autism

There was a pattern in clinical psychology in that you were asked to look at two mental health issues by looking at their symptoms and features, explanations for them, and treatments. This pattern of considering a disorder is repeated here regarding **autism**. However, 'symptoms' are not appropriate and 'therapy' rather than 'treatment' is focused on because it is about helping a child with autism rather than dealing with a mental health issue.

Features of autism

Autism spectrum disorder (ASD) is disorder from Asperger syndrome, which is mild autism, to severe autism. Boys are more affected by autism than girls, by about four boys to one girl. About one to two people in every 1,000 have autism, or from 0.1% to 0.2% of the population. Features include finding it hard to read the emotions of others and finding communication and forming relationships very difficult.

One biological explanation for autism

Autism has been said to be an extreme 'male brain' condition because females tend to have high empathising and males tend to be high systematisers. Females are better at reading body language too, which those with autism find very difficult.

One other explanation for autism: a cognitive explanation

Theory of mind is a cognitive explanation of autism. Autism seems to mean not being able to see someone else's viewpoint, such as not knowing that others cannot know what the person with autism knows or is thinking. This is not having 'theory of mind'. There is **low empathising** and **high systematising**, which are features of cognitive processing.

Links

Individual differences link

There are differences between children with autism with regard to their characteristics.

Developmental psychology

Autism is a developmental disorder in that it affects a child's development.

Exam tip

Use van Ijzendoorn and Kroonenberg (1988) (page 45) and Cassibba et al. (2013) (page 45) when discussing the universality of attachment types and nature–nurture issues, including the use of cross-cultural comparisons as well as meta-analysis.

Exam tip

This material on attachment types, and cross-cultural studies suggesting attachment types are universals, is useful for the nature–nurture issues and debate. It is worth reading through the material you have to cover in your course to pick out where material can suit your issues and debates.

Exam tip

When there are two theories asked for in your course, such as two explanations of autism, you could learn comparison points. This is a good way to learn a theory as well as to focus on evaluation. Make notes comparing the two explanations for autism you focus on.

Therapies for helping children with autism

Applied behaviour analysis (ABA)

ABA focuses on play and social behaviour, communication and living skills, with the aim of improving them. The aim is to look at challenging behaviours and teach more appropriate forms of behaviour to help someone with autism in their daily life. Token economy is part of ABA, and involves rewarding appropriate behaviour using operant conditioning principles.

Pivotal response training (PRT)

PRT was developed as contemporary ABA. It gives the child more control of activities and the teacher–child interactions are more spontaneous. There is less careful planning and interactions involving the rewarding of appropriate behaviour are more natural, which makes this a different therapy.

Individual differences

The importance of individual differences has been noted in the above content section for child psychology. In summary, parenting style and temperament relate to someone's individuality, and Thomas and Chess suggest babies can be 'difficult', 'easy', or 'fearful', which is their temperament (for life). A certain type of day care can affect a child differently according to their temperament, which shows the importance of individual differences in children, and autism and such developmental issues lead to differences in individual children.

Developmental psychology

The importance of issues for our development has been noted in the above content section for child psychology. In summary, child psychology relates clearly to development, such as how the effects of privation and deprivation on a child, including maternal deprivation, affect their relationships including later ones. Day care has been shown to affect children's development, depending on its quality, and autism is a developmental disorder that affects a child's development.

Methods

Observation

Types of observation

Participant and non-participant

Participant observations are where the person gathering the data has a role in the situation being observed and is part of it. **Non-participant observation** is where the observer is separate from what is being observed; they are not participating.

Overt and covert

Overt observations are where the participants know about the observation. **Covert observations** are where the observation is done secretly; the participants are not aware they are part of an observation.

Exam tip

You covered operant conditioning in learning theories. Rewards must be something a child wants, and there must be careful planning looking at the antecedent (what goes before the behaviour), the behaviour itself and the consequences of the child's behaviour. Remind yourself about Skinner's ideas if you need to.

Exam tip

If using ABA and PRT, which are different therapies, be sure to present them sufficiently differently by focusing on differences, such as the naturalness of PRT and the child having more control of the therapy. In any exam answer be sure to show explicitly that you are answering the question.

Knowledge check 31

Why do you think PRT was developed as 'contemporary ABA', focusing more on giving the child control?

Qualitative and quantitative data

Qualitative data are in words, pictures, photographs or songs — where data are 'quality' rather than numbers. Quantitative data are numbers, such as percentages or ratings using self-report data.

Tallying

Tallying is used to get quantitative data in an observation and involves making a mark when a particular behaviour is observed, such as a girl smoking.

Questionnaire and interview

Questionnaire

Open and closed questions

Open questions gather qualitative data and enable the respondent to write freely. Closed questions gather quantitative number and have a 'closed' choice of answers, such as ranking on a scale of 0 to 5, rating on a Likert scale ('strongly disagree' to 'strongly agree'), or 'yes'/'no' answers. **Closed questions** are limiting but easier to analyse and compare. 'Questions' can be 'items' and do not always have a question mark.

> **Knowledge check 32**
>
> Which out of qualitative or quantitative data would the following two items/ questions generate? Which is an open question?
> a What do you think about children smoking?
> b Rate your opinion of children smoking using 0 for don't mind to 5 for very concerned.

Sampling

You have looked at random, volunteer, opportunity and stratified sampling.

Demand characteristics

If a respondent can see what is wanted in a study, such as a questionnaire being obvious in its intent, they might respond accordingly, which means their answers are biased. This is called **demand characteristics**.

Social desirability

If a respondent answers in a way they think is wanted in a society rather than giving their own ideas, this is **social desirability** and a form of bias.

> **Exam tip**
>
> You have already come across a lot of the terms in this application. Review your learning of them. You will be reviewing them for the psychological skills part of your course (Student Guide 4) so you will have the chance to revise the meaning of terms then too.

> **Exam tip**
>
> It is useful to use qualitative versus quantitative data when evaluating research methods. In general, qualitative data will have a validity that quantitative data do not, and quantitative data will show replicability and reliability that qualitative data will not.

> **Exam tip**
>
> You can be asked to write a suitable closed or open question in a given scenario. It is useful to give an example that requires a question mark. For closed questions, be sure that you give the choice (e.g. 'yes'/'no') so that you present the item as a question.

> **Exam tip**
>
> Sampling was reviewed in criminological psychology. Check your understanding, including strengths and weaknesses of the different techniques.

Interview

Structured, unstructured and semi-structured interviews

Structured interview means having set questions, **unstructured interview** means an open schedule that an interviewee can guide, and **semi-structured interview** means a schedule to guide but the interviewer can still go with an interviewee's responses.

Cross-cultural research

The use of meta-analysis using cross-cultural research and the universality of attachment types

Cross-cultural research as a method was looked at in clinical psychology (page 19), as was **meta-analysis** (page 19). The classic study in child psychology uses a cross-cultural approach and meta-analysis, as does Cassibba et al. (2013) (page 45). If attachment types are found in all cultures (where they are studied), that suggests a **universality** of attachment types, which means they are down to human nature and not to learning.

The Strange Situation

See page 37 where this procedure is covered.

Cross-sectional versus longitudinal designs

See page 19 in clinical psychology for coverage of these two designs.

Nature–nurture issues

Cross-cultural studies can uncover nature issues because if something is found in all cultures it is thought of as being in human nature. Cultures tend to nurture differently and so nurture would show differences between cultures.

The ethics of researching with children

You have come across ethics a lot in your course, including the BPS *Code of Ethics and Conduct* (2009). Researching and working with children has special ethical considerations.

UNCRC (1989)

The United Nations Convention on the Rights of the Child (UNCRC) in 1989 adopted a list of articles for how children (up to the age of 18 years) must be treated.

Participation and protection

An important part of the UNCRC is the right for children to participate in research about them, so research should be 'with' children rather than 'on' or 'about' children. Children also have the right to be protected, which can go against their right to participate.

> **Exam tip**
>
> Prepare examples to use when discussing issues, such as a study looking at autism to illustrate the need to protect the child but also to give them their participation rights. An example can help to illustrate the difficulties and to show understanding.

> **Exam tip**
>
> Use the classic study and Cassibba et al. (2013) as examples of cross-cultural research and meta-analyses and use them to see what these two research approaches are.

> **Exam tip**
>
> Be ready to use the methodology in this application appropriately, such as cross-cultural studies in child psychology (e.g. attachment types) and longitudinal designs in child psychology (e.g. following a child's language development).

> **Knowledge check 33**
>
> Give an example of an area of study where it might be hard to give full participation rights because of wanting to protect a child.

Analysis of data

You need to look at analysis of quantitative data, as explained in clinical psychology (page 20). You also need to cover analysis of qualitative data, focusing on thematic analysis and grounded theory, as in clinical psychology.

Studies

Classic study: van Ijzendoorn and Kroonenberg (1988)

van Ijzendoorn and Kroonenberg (1988) compared findings from studies using the Strange Situation in different cultures to see how far there are universals in attachment types. They did find that secure attachment (Type B) was always the largest type, suggesting universality. They found differences too, however, such as more Type C in Israel and Japan and more Type A in Western European countries.

Contemporary study: Cassibba et al. (2013)

You have three contemporary studies to choose from. They are Cassibba et al. (2013), Gagnon-Oosterwaal et al. (2012) and Li et al. (2013). Cassibba et al. (2013) is summarised here. However, if you have studied one of the other two, you might prefer to revise your own chosen study. Your textbook will give you more detail.

Cassibba et al. (2013) includes van Ijzendoorn in the team and links well with the classic study, as it is also a meta-analysis focusing on the same area. Cassibba et al. (2013) found attachment types in Italy very similar to the spread of those in the US norm that was being used, which links to Ainsworth's Baltimore study (page 41). They found some differences between cultures as well, suggesting attachment types have some environmental basis.

> **Exam tip**
>
> One way of learning studies is to compare them. Make a list of evaluation issues (e.g. validity and reliability) and compare the two studies given here to note similarities and differences and in readiness for evaluating them. The two studies are, of course, very similar, having similar research questions.

> **Questions & Answers**
>
> Option applications Studies Q1 asks about the aims of van Ijzendoorn and Kroonenberg (1988) and of Cassibba et al. (2013).

Key question

You need to know about one key question which concepts and research in child psychology can explain. The question must be important to today's society. One key question is looked at in this book. However, you may have studied another one and might prefer to revise that one.

> **Exam tip**
>
> Be ready to answer a question about analysis of qualitative data in as much detail as you would discuss analysis of quantitative data. You could have a scenario given in a question that required you to discuss the analysis of qualitative data, for example.

> **Exam tip**
>
> van Ijzendoorn and Kroonenberg (1988) used meta-analysis of cross-cultural studies and so is a useful study when looking at method issues in child psychology in your course.

> **Knowledge check 34**
>
> Studies using the Strange Situation and looking for universality of attachment types tend to use the US norm, based on Ainsworth's Baltimore study. What is this 'norm'?

What issues should parents take into account when deciding about day care for their child?

Describing the question

It seems that parents are concerned about leaving their child in someone else's care. However, there is a desire or need for parents to work, both to suit their own circumstances and for society to have people in the workforce. An option for society might be to pay parents to bring up children, except that that would not suit the workforce requirements. The key question here is how psychology can inform parents about what issues they need to consider when choosing day care for their child if day care is deemed to be necessary. Day care has been shown to be advantageous but also not so advantageous.

Concepts, theories and research from child psychology in your course

Explaining what issues parents should take into account when deciding about day care for their child

In general the issues parents need to consider seem to be: the quality of the day care; how old their child is and, depending on that, how long they would leave the child in day care per day and per week; the qualifications of the staff; the adult-to-child ratio, which should be low; and the facilities offered.

> **Exam tip**
>
> Use the answers to the knowledge checks to help with your learning. You could make notes from the knowledge check answers and find ways to use them in your revision. For example, look at the knowledge check answers without the question and see if you can work the question out, then check.

Practical investigation

You will have carried out a practical within child psychology if you chose this option, using a questionnaire, interview or observation. Go back over your notes to revise what you did.

Some general ideas about the practical and what to learn

You have to carry out a questionnaire, an interview or an observation based on the child psychology material in your course. You can collect qualitative or quantitative data but will need to turn qualitative into quantitative if you have no directly quantitative data. This is because you need to use the appropriate statistical test from the four in your course to analyse your data. You need to include a research question and/or hypothesis, the research method, sampling, ethical considerations, data collection tools, data analysis, results and discussion. You should also look at the strengths and weaknesses of the practical and at possible improvements.

> **Exam tip**
>
> Avoid describing the key question using the psychology about the pros and cons of day care and *issues* around good and poor quality day care. That material goes into the part where you *explain* the key question using concepts from child psychology. In this part, *describe why* this is a key question for society.

> **Exam tip**
>
> What is given here is a summary of the issues. You need to consider concepts (such as separation anxiety and deprivation), theories (such as Bowlby's material deprivation hypothesis) and research (such as Belsky and Pluess, 2011, on child temperament).

> **Knowledge check 35**
>
> Suggest why parents would want to choose day care for their child carefully.

Exam tip

Practise using these ideas as questions and prepare answers. For example, write about ideas for improving your study, the strengths and weaknesses of it, the data collection tools and your analysis, with the results.

Issues and debates

Issues and debates are discussed in Student Guide 4, as they are part of psychological skills as well as being threaded through the topic areas in your course.

Summary: child psychology

- Child psychology covers attachment, deprivation and privation, including Bowlby's and Ainsworth's ideas and the Strange Situation procedure.
- Research into deprivation and how negative effects might be reduced, and research into privation and whether negative effects can be reversed, are included.
- Research into day care, including advantages and disadvantages as well as what makes good and poor quality day care, is covered.
- Cross-cultural research into attachment types and nature–nurture issues, which are also covered by the classic study (van Ijzendoorn and Kroonenberg, 1988) and one of the contemporary studies (Cassibba et al., 2013), are required.
- Features, explanations and therapies for autism are required.
- Observation, interview and questionnaire are the main research methods, as well as cross-cultural research methods and meta-analysis.

- The ethics of researching with children are covered, including the UNCRC and children's rights of protection and participation.
- Analysis of qualitative data using thematic analysis and grounded theory, and analysis of quantitative data using issues, as found in clinical psychology.
- The classic study is van Ijzendoorn and Kroonenberg (1988) and one of the contemporary studies is Cassibba et al. (2013), the one covered in this guide. There are two other contemporary studies you can choose.
- A key question is what issues should parents take into account when choosing day care for their child.
- The practical application must be an interview, a questionnaire or an observation and there must be analysis using the required inferential statistical test as well as understanding of various research issues, strengths and weaknesses of the study and ideas for improvements.

■ Health psychology

This section looks at health psychology (an option application). Sections on criminological psychology and child psychology are found elsewhere in this guide. You will have studied one of these three applications, so focus on the one you have studied. Clinical psychology is worth 54 of the 90 marks in Paper 3 and has been given more focus in this guide.

Table 24 Summary of health psychology in your course

Content
Issues around drug taking, including addiction, tolerance, physical and psychological dependency and withdrawal. A biological explanation (including mode of action) and a learning explanation of drug addictions, two treatments for drug addictions and one anti-drug campaign. Explanations and treatments focus on alcohol, heroin and nicotine.
As in other topic areas, individual differences and developmental psychology need to be linked into the content studied.
Methodology
The use of animals to study drugs in lab experiments and the ethics of doing this, as well as two research methods using humans to study drugs and the ethics of doing this. The use of cross-cultural research to look at drug misuse and nature–nurture issues, and data analysis issues, as in clinical psychology.
Two studies in detail
Olds and Milner (1954), the classic study, and Pengpid et al. (2013), a contemporary study, are described and evaluated. You may have studied Mundt et al. (2012) or Dixit et al. (2012) as your contemporary study instead.
Key question
How to encourage the cessation of smoking is chosen as the key question here, but you may have looked at one or more different key questions.
Practical
You will have carried out at least one practical in health psychology and you should use your own investigation, because you will have 'learned by doing'. Some ideas about the practical are suggested in this guide.

> **Exam tip**
>
> Be ready for questions that ask you about health psychology in general, such as that it is about understanding health from a social, biological and cognitive basis as well as being about promoting good health.

> **Exam tip**
>
> Use this table to draw up a checklist of what you need to cover in your revision. Annotate it to show what you feel you know (green tick), what just needs some brief revision (amber circle) and which areas you cannot remember much about (red cross).

Issues around drug taking

Addiction

Addiction is about being physically and psychologically dependent on a drug. It refers to not meeting family and work commitments, as well as the body and mind being dependent. Addiction is about the compulsion to take the drug and an obsession with getting a supply of the drug.

Tolerance

Tolerance is a feature of drug taking, being the need to take increasing amounts of a drug to get the same effect as was first achieved. The body adapts to the drug and so the effect is lessened, which means taking more to get the same 'high'.

Physical dependency

The body becomes used to functioning with the drug in the system so the drug is needed for 'normal' functioning of the brain and body. Tolerance is produced. This **physical dependency** also means that there are withdrawal symptoms if the drug taking is stopped.

Psychological dependency

Psychological dependency means the drug is very important in someone's life and cravings are hard to resist. The drug is important to the person's mental state — psychological dependency relates to the compulsion the person might feel to take the drug and to their motivation to do so. Withdrawal symptoms are to do with not feeling pleasure once the drug taking is stopped, and feeling anxiety.

Withdrawal

Withdrawal refers to the physical symptoms that are experienced once the drug is stopped; such symptoms differ, depending on the drug.

Explanations of drug addiction

Biological explanations: alcohol, heroin and nicotine addiction

Neuronal/**synaptic transmission** using neurotransmitters is a common explanation for drug addiction. Drugs are chemicals and act like **neurotransmitters** at the synapse. Different drugs act in different ways but the basics are the same.

Biological explanation for alcohol addiction

Alcohol affects **receptor sites** in the brain, at the synapse, specifically **dopamine** receptors. When there is more dopamine in the brain's reward pathways this gives a pleasure response. Alcohol reduces glutamate activity at the NDMA glutamate receptor and also increases the inhibiting effect of GABA at the $GABA_A$ receptor.

Links

Individual differences link

As with biological explanations of other issues such as mental disorders, the focus is on everyone's brain working in the same way, so there is little room for individual differences. However, there might be individual differences in people's biology (or their personality perhaps) that affect their drug-taking behaviour.

Biological explanation for heroin addiction

Heroin works in the brain like morphine and acts on opioid receptors. Heroin causes changes at the receptors. It changes the action of dopamine in the reward pathways, releasing more dopamine than usual, hence the 'high'.

Exam tip

By learning the definitions of the terms you will find you can explain them as well, partly because the issues often overlap. Physical dependency, for example, is shown by there being withdrawal symptoms when the drug taking is stopped.

Knowledge check 36

What is the difference between withdrawal and tolerance?

Exam tip

Use what you learned about neurotransmitter functioning in biological and clinical psychology to help with understanding biological explanations for alcohol, heroin and nicotine addiction.

Biological explanation for nicotine addiction

Nicotine works at nicotinic receptors in the nervous system, inhibiting the function of nicotinic acetylcholine receptors — it stimulates the acetylcholine receptor and then blocks it. This helps memory. Levels of acetylcholine remain in the gap, affecting mood, such as reducing anxiety. This occurs through the release of dopamine triggered by the effect of nicotine on the acetylcholine receptors. In other words, like heroin, nicotine affects dopamine in the reward systems of the brain.

Learning explanations: alcohol, heroin and nicotine addiction

Operant conditioning principles suggest that people do again what they are rewarded for doing. If drugs produce a pleasure response, that can be rewarding, so the drug is taken again. **Social learning** suggests people imitate behaviour they see rewarded, so if someone else is rewarded by taking drugs, and is a role model, their drug-taking behaviour may be copied. **Classical conditioning** principles suggest that if a natural response, such as pleasure in response to a drug, is paired with something in the environment (e.g. drug-related cues) then the environmental cues can lead to the pleasure response and could maintain drug taking by people staying near their 'cues'.

Learning explanation for alcohol addiction

Social learning is about observation of a role model and then, if there is motivation to do so, repetition of the observed behaviour. This learning can apply to drug addiction, including alcohol addiction.

Learning explanation for heroin addiction

Tolerance can relate to cues in the environment that trigger heroin-related physical reactions. Without the cues, the tolerance reaction (needs a larger dose) might not happen, and so the larger dose of heroin would have a stronger effect, which can be dangerous — this happened in rats (Siegel et al., 1982). This suggests that cues relate to drug taking. The pleasure from the drug might be cued from the environment, which might trigger drug-taking behaviour by giving a reminder.

Learning explanation for nicotine addiction

The idea of drugs being positively reinforcing applies to all drugs, including nicotine, as there is a rewarding effect in the brain's reward pathways.

Links

Developmental psychology link

Learning theories relate drug taking to environmental cues and features, which affect a person's development. Someone can become involved in drug taking through it being rewarded, which affects their development through life.

Knowledge check 37

Referring to biological explanations, why do you think — though drugs act differently at the synapse depending on the drug — there is the common factor that they produce pleasure and a 'high'?

Exam tip

Relate your understanding of learning theories to learning explanations for drug misuse.

Exam tip

Social learning is suggested here to explain alcohol addiction, with classical conditioning linked to heroin addiction and operant conditioning linked to nicotine addiction. However, the three learning explanations can apply to each of the different drugs.

Knowledge check 38

If an explanation refers to a) association with cues, b) copying someone's rewarded behaviour or c) doing again what is rewarding, which of the three learning theories is referred to in each of these explanations?

Treatments for alcohol, heroin and nicotine addiction

Two treatments for alcohol addiction

Drug therapy

Drugs can be used in the detoxification stage of overcoming alcohol addiction. Drugs that have been used are naltrexone, disulfiram, antidepressants and benzodiazepines. Disulfiram stops liver enzymes from breaking down acetaldehyde, which is toxic and leads to nausea, sweating and headaches when someone drinks alcohol.

> **Links**
>
> **Individual differences link**
>
> People do react to acetaldehyde differently, so disulfiram in its standard dose might not work for everyone, showing there are individual differences in reactions to therapies.

Aversion therapy

Aversion therapy can be used for drug addiction. Disulfiram (Antabuse) is used to prevent relapse and sensitises people to alcohol. Its use can be explained using classical conditioning principles. The use of Antabuse can be seen as a drug therapy *and* a learning theory therapy. Disulfiram leads to unpleasant symptoms if alcohol is drunk and to avoid unpleasant symptoms someone stops drinking the alcohol. They learn an aversion to alcohol. Alcohol is associated with the nausea and sickness and so is avoided.

Two treatments for heroin addiction

Drug therapy

Prescribing heroin or a substitute that works in the same way as heroin, such as methadone, a synthetic opiate, is a treatment for heroin addiction. Methadone blocks the effects of heroin at the synapse and removes withdrawal symptoms. Without withdrawal symptoms, giving up the drug is more likely. Buprenorphine is another drug used to treat heroin, a weaker opiate than methadone with lower levels of physical dependence.

CBT

CBT focuses on thinking, emotions and behaviour and is used to prevent relapse, not just for heroin, but for other drugs too. CBT can look at the positive and negative consequences of drug taking for the individual and at dysfunctional thinking that might be involved.

Questions & Answers

Option applications Content Q2 asks about drug therapy for heroin addiction.

Exam tip

You can choose the two therapies for each of the three drugs, though one of the therapies you choose must be aversion therapy. You can use one therapy for more than one of the drugs if that is appropriate. However, be sure to focus the therapy on the particular drug.

Exam tip

You have probably used CBT as a therapy elsewhere in your course, such as for depression, OCD or anorexia in clinical psychology. Use what you know about the therapy and apply it to the different issues. In this guide CBT is used for schizophrenia (pages 16–17) and for depression (page 18).

Two treatments for nicotine addiction

Drug therapy

Nicotine replacement therapy can be seen as drug therapy because the drug nicotine is given in patches or gum to help with stopping smoking. Varenicline tartrate can be used for withdrawal symptoms too, though it can cause nausea.

Treatment based on classical conditioning principles

Cue-exposure therapy relates to classical conditioning principles. In the therapy, cues related to smoking are presented; this can be a 'virtual' presentation. While not smoking, the person is exposed to the cues and in time the association between cues and smoking should be extinguished.

Links

Developmental psychology link

Learning theories relate to development because they show how people develop behaviour through associations and rewards as well as through observational learning.

Exam tip

Stopping smoking is the key question chosen in this guide for health psychology and you can use this material to discuss the key question.

Knowledge check 39

Relate cue-exposure therapy to classical conditioning principles.

One anti-drug campaign and the psychological strategies behind it

One campaign is the Toxic Cycle Health Harms campaign in December 2013, which came from the British Heart Foundation and showed the harm smoking can do by using strong images to shock people. The advertising achieved 87% awareness and 30% of those who saw the campaign took action regarding stopping smoking.

Psychological strategies behind the campaign

Social learning theory is used, such as a man seen smoking outside his workplace and then showing the harm smoking does to his body, targeting men in a similar work situation. Of people seeing the advert, 84% said it was targeted at people like them, so the campaign seemed to be successful in putting forward appropriate role models to encourage social learning.

Self-efficacy is an idea that people have to believe they can change for change to happen and a 'fear' campaign will not do that, a 'hope' part of the campaign is also needed.

Links

Individual differences link

Learning theories like social learning theory may apply to everyone in principle but what is learned, what is reinforced and what is copied can depend on individuals and their interactions with their environment.

Exam tip

The specification asks you to know about one anti-drug campaign and here smoking is used. You also have to look at the psychological strategies behind the campaign. Use the specification, which you can find using the Edexcel website, to check exactly what you need to cover.

Knowledge check 40

Give three aspects of social learning theory that are likely to be used in anti-drug television campaigns.

Individual differences

The importance of individual differences has been noted in the above content section for health psychology. In summary, there might be individual differences in people's biology, such as their personality, that might affect their drug-taking behaviour. People encounter different experiences when learning, such as imitating specific role models, so everyone's learning will be individual and affect people differently. Also people react to drugs differently, such as acetaldehyde, and not everyone will respond to one drug in the same way.

Developmental psychology

The importance of issues for our development has been noted in the above content section for health psychology. In summary, learning theories explain drug-taking by showing how environmental cues can affect people's behaviour. People develop behaviour through associations, rewards and observational learning, which in turn affect their development.

Methods

Use of animals in lab experiments to study drugs

Laboratory experiments, including those where animals are used, have features relating to psychology as a science, including having careful **controls** over all variables except the **independent variable** — the **IV** — (which is manipulated) and the **dependent variable** — the **DV** — (which is measured to see changes from the manipulation of the IV). If there are no **confounding variables** (variables not controlled for) then cause-and-effect conclusions can be drawn relating to the hypothesis.

Using animals in experiments gives more control because animals can be manipulated, such as using lesions to damage their brain in specific areas to see the effect on drug taking. Olds and Milner (1954), the classic study in health psychology, used electrical stimulation to see which brain regions related to rewards in rats.

> **Exam tip**
>
> Prepare studies as examples. If you used van den Oever et al. (2008) as a contemporary study in biological psychology, that was about drug taking, environmental cues and extinction. Use your learning in Year 1 and apply it when considering the applications for Paper 2.

Ethics of using animals to study drugs

The Animals (Scientific Procedures) Act 1986 gives rules about using animals in laboratory experiments and the rules are backed by Home Office licensing.

> **Exam tip**
>
> Check your understanding of the rules for using animals, such as the researcher having a licence, the place where the study is carried out also having a licence, as well as the animals being the right ones and not endangered and so on.

Exam tip

Check your understanding of the terms relating to experiments in psychology. They are reviewed in Student Guide 4, which focuses on psychological skills, so you have another chance to revise them.

Knowledge check 41

Briefly explain two animal studies that used laboratory experimental methods. They do not have to be animal studies that look at drug taking.

Exam tip

You will need examples of studies that use animals to study drugs. Check the specification to make sure you know exactly what you can be assessed on.

Exam tip

When evaluating the use of animals in lab experiments to study drugs, make sure you separate out practical strengths and weaknesses from ethical strengths and weaknesses and make sure you answer a question appropriately. Avoid using 'human' ethical principles when discussing the use of animals.

Two research methods using humans to study drugs

Randomised controlled trials using human participants to study drugs

One method using humans to research drugs is **randomised controlled trials (RCTs)**. There is a **treatment group** and a **control group**. The control group can be a waiting list group — a group waiting for the treatment, so that someone is not deprived of a potentially effective treatment. **Placebo** controlled trials are where a participant is either given the drug of interest or a placebo (a sugar pill, perhaps). The placebo group is the control group.

In RCTs there can be a **single-blind procedure** (the participant does not know what group they are in) or a **double-blind procedure** (when neither the participant nor the person running the study knows whether the participant is in a placebo/treatment group or not).

> **Exam tip**
>
> Pengpid et al. (2013) used an RCT to look at the effectiveness of a brief intervention relating to alcohol consumption. This is the contemporary study given in this guide for this application. You can use it as an example of RCT use.

Interviews using human participants to study drugs

Dixit et al. (2012), one of the contemporary studies in your course in health psychology, used interviewing to gather their data about attitudes to alcohol use in India. 'There are three types of interview: **structured**, **unstructured** and **semi-structured** (see page 44).

> **Exam tip**
>
> For health psychology, draw on what you learned about using interviewing to gather data in social psychology. However, when giving examples, remember to use examples from health psychology relating to studying drug usage.

Ethics when using human participants to study drugs

You have already covered the ethics of researching using human participants, in social psychology and elsewhere in this guide. Draw on your understanding, including the BPS *Code of Ethics and Conduct* (2009) and issues around risk management.

The use of cross-cultural research related to drug misuse, including nature–nurture issues

Cross-cultural research methods were covered in clinical psychology in your course, including looking at how they relate to nature and nurture issues in human characteristics. Culture, for example, can guide beliefs about drug misuse and attitudes to treatment as well as diagnosis of substance use disorders.

> **Knowledge check 42**
>
> What is the purpose of the 'randomised' bit of randomised controlled trials?

> **Exam tip**
>
> Where possible, use such terms as single- and double-blind, and waiting list controls, to show understanding of issues.

> **Knowledge check 43**
>
> What is the purpose of the control group in RTCs?

> **Knowledge check 44**
>
> What are the advantages of using interviewing rather than lab experiments when using human participants to study drugs?

> **Exam tip**
>
> Nature–nurture is one of the issues and debates in your course. It is reviewed in Student Guide 4, which looks at psychological skills, so you can review the debate then. Use what you covered in clinical psychology (page 19) to review what is meant by 'universality'.

Analysis of data

You need to look at analysis of quantitative data as explained in clinical psychology (page 20). You also need to cover analysis of qualitative data focusing on thematic analysis and grounded theory, as in clinical psychology.

Studies

Classic study: Olds and Milner (1954)

Olds and Milner (1954), using electrical stimulation and animal experiments, found rats would press more when certain brain areas were stimulated and they concluded these were pleasure areas in the brain.

Contemporary study: Pengpid et al. (2013)

You have three contemporary studies to choose from. They are Mundt et al. (2012), Dixit et al. (2012) and Pengpid et al. (2013). Pengpid et al. (2013) is summarised here. If you have studied one of the other two, you might prefer to revise your own chosen study. Your textbook will give you more detail.

Pengpid et al. (2013) focused on therapy for alcohol misuse using a single-blinded randomised controlled trial, and so is useful for method as well as for the results. They found that the brief intervention for alcohol addiction was not significantly effective compared with the control group.

> **Exam tip**
>
> Use studies as examples of methods (such as RCTs) and also to relate to therapy (such as Pengpid et al.'s, 2013, brief intervention). Make use of what you know when it comes to answering questions.

Key question

You need to know about one key question which concepts and research in health psychology can explain. The question must be important to today's society. One key question is looked at in this book. However, you may have studied another one and might prefer to revise that one.

How to encourage the cessation of smoking

Describing the question

As seen when considering one anti-drug campaign, smoking relates to poor health, including heart attack, so from an economic point of view society would do well to encourage people to stop smoking. For the person themselves, it is an unhealthy habit. Nicotine is addictive and affects dopamine pathways in the brain and brain functioning, so stopping smoking would help the individual as well. As nicotine is an addictive drug, stopping smoking might not be done without encouragement.

Exam tip

Be ready to answer a question about analysis of qualitative data in as much detail as you would discuss analysis of quantitative data. You could have a scenario given in a question that required you to discuss the analysis of qualitative data, for example.

Exam tip

You can use Olds and Milner (1954) as an example of animal laboratory research and also to discuss relevant ethical issues.

Knowledge check 45

Make three comparison points between Olds and Milner (1954) and Pengpid et al. (2013).

Exam tip

It is important to describe the issue itself, such as why it is a problem for society or the individual. Here it is not just 'smoking' or 'nicotine use' that is the issue, but how it can be stopped (and perhaps why society would want it stopped).

Concepts, theories and research from health psychology in your course

Explaining issues around encouraging stopping of smoking

You can use explanations for nicotine addiction to show why stopping is hard, for example neurotransmitter and/or learning explanations, such as how smoking might be a learned habit which is hard to break.

Questions & Answers

Option applications Key question Q1 asks about two concepts relating to a key question in health psychology.

Practical investigation

You will have carried out a practical within health psychology if you chose this option. You may have used a questionnaire, an interview or a content analysis. Go back over your notes to revise what you did.

Some general ideas about the practical and what to learn

You have to use interview, questionnaire or content analysis. You need to use quantitative data, which can come from categorising qualitative data, because you need to use one of the four inferential tests in your course to analyse your data. You need to include a research question and/or hypothesis, the research method, sampling, ethical considerations, data collection tools, data analysis, results and discussion. You should also look at the strengths and weaknesses of the practical and at possible improvements.

Issues and debates

Issues and debates are discussed in Student Guide 4, as they are part of psychological skills as well as being threaded through the topic areas in your course.

> **Exam tip**
>
> Prepare concepts such as ideas around neurotransmitter functioning, and theories such as classical and operant conditioning, as well as studies such as Olds and Milner, to show how drugs can give pleasure, which is then pursued by not giving the drug up.

> **Exam tip**
>
> Practise using these points as questions and prepare answers. For example, write out your research question and be ready to explain the result of your inferential statistical testing and whether you accepted or rejected your null hypothesis.

Summary: health psychology

- Issues around drug taking, including addiction, tolerance, physical and psychological dependence and withdrawal, are required.
- One biological explanation each for alcohol, heroin and nicotine is required, including in each case the mode of action; and one learning explanation each for alcohol, heroin and nicotine is required.
- Two treatments each for alcohol, heroin and nictoine are required. One of the treatments must be aversion therapy.
- One anti-drug campaign and the psychological strategies behind it is required.
- You need to know about the use of animals in lab experiments to study drugs and two research methods that use humans to study drugs, including the ethical issues when doing research (for both).

- Cross-cultural research related to drug misuse, including nature–nurture issues, is required.
- Data analysis issues relating to qualitative and quantitative data, as in clinical psychology, is required.
- You need to know the classic study for health psychology, which is Olds and Milner (1954), a lab experimental animal study looking at the function of different brain regions, and one from a list of three contemporary studies — Pengpid et al. (2013) is chosen here.
- How to encourage stopping smoking is a key question for society.
- You need to carry out an interview, a questionnaire or a content analysis as a practical investigation.

Questions & Answers

Introduction

This section follows the structure of the course, with questions on clinical psychology first and then questions on the option applications.

The clinical psychology questions follow the course structure too — overview of the topic, content, methods, studies, key question, practical, and issues and debates, as shown in the table below.

For the option applications questions the same structure is followed, though the actual questions and answers may come from any of the three options. Taken together they provide a range from the three applications to give you an idea of what sort of questions to look out for and how answers might be written and marked.

There is no issues and debates question in option applications, but one such question is included in clinical psychology to remind you that issues and debates questions do come up in Paper 2. Student Guide 4 focuses on issues and debates.

Table 1 Questions offered in each section

Clinical psychology	Number of questions	Option applications	Number of questions
Overview	1	Overview	1
Content	3	Content	2
Methods	1	Methods	1
Studies	2	Studies	1
Key question	1	Key question	1
Practical	1	Practical	1
Issues and debates	1		

The example questions can be used as practice questions for A-level Paper 2, and for the methods section of A-level Paper 3.

Examiner's comments

All questions and answers are followed by examiner's comments. These are preceded by the icon **e** or **e**. They indicate what a question requires, where credit is due, strengths in the answer, areas for improvement, specific problems, common errors, lack of clarity, irrelevance, mistakes in the meaning of terms and/or misinterpretation of the question. The comments also indicate how the answers might be marked in an exam — there are ticks in the answers to show where exactly marks are awarded.

Examination issues

Assessment objectives

You are marked according to assessment objectives (AOs). You can find these in the specification, but they are summarised here:

- **AO1** — knowledge with understanding of scientific ideas, processes, techniques and procedures (knowing and understanding)
- **AO2** — applying knowledge and understanding of scientific ideas, processes, techniques and procedures (applying)
- **AO3** — analysing, interpreting and evaluating a range of scientific information, ideas and evidence to make judgements and reach conclusions and also to refine practical design and procedures (commenting)

A good plan is to consider the exam paper as covering the three AOs in equal proportions (one third each) and to consider the four topic areas and sections within them to be evenly covered. That will help you when preparing.

Exam questions and marking

Your A-level exams will have some points-based marking and some levels-based marking:

- up to 8 marks is likely to mean points-based, which means 1 mark for each point clearly made
- 8 marks and over is likely to be levels marking, which means a mark depending on where in bands the answer fits

A-level Paper 2: Expect short-answer questions that are points-based, also some 8-mark questions and, at the end of each topic, a 16-mark or 20-mark question on issues and debates (extended writing uses levels marking). You do clinical psychology and one of the other three topics. Questions on each topic are given in topic order (Topics 5 to 8), with the extended writing at the end of each topic. Content regarding issues and debates is covered in Student Guide 4, not in this guide, though an issues and debates question is given in the clinical psychology area to show they can occur in Paper 2.

A-level Paper 3: Some of the short-answer method questions in this guide can suit A-level Paper 3, as can some of the questions on studies. Where a question suits Paper 3, this is noted.

Extended open-response questions: allocation of AOs

The different mark allocations for extended open-response questions have different assessment objective splits. This is worth knowing about. Extended open-response questions are from 8 marks onwards:

- 8 marks can be split into: AO1 4 marks and AO2* 4 marks; or AO1 4 marks and AO3 4 marks
- 12 marks can be split into: AO1 4 marks, AO2* 4 marks and AO3 4 marks; or AO1 6 marks and AO3 6 marks

- 16 marks can be split into: AO1 6 marks, AO2* 4 marks and AO3 6 marks; or AO1 6 marks and AO3 10 marks
- 20 marks can be split into: AO1 8 marks, AO2* 4 marks and AO3 8 marks; or AO1 8 marks and AO3 12 marks

*You will know if you need to focus on AO2 (applying your knowledge and understanding) because there will be a scenario of some sort to apply it to and a comment about you needing to refer to the scenario. Without a scenario to apply your knowledge and understanding to, the marks will be AO1 and AO3 with the splits as outlined here. AO2 always has 4 marks, as you can see.

Interpreting question command words

Questions have one command word, such as 'describe', 'assess' or 'calculate'. Appendix 6 in the specification lists the command words and what you have to do for each. Use the Appendix to generate your own questions and make sure you do what is asked. For example, 'evaluate', 'assess', 'to what extent' and 'explain' all require you to come to a judgement in some way, or a conclusion.

How to use this section

- Revise clinical psychology and your chosen 'other' applications area using this guide and your other books/notes.
- Work through the questions, answering each one yourself without reading the advice on how to answer the question and without reading the answer given. If the question here relates to a different option application from the one you have studied, substitute a similar question using material from your chosen application. Suggestions are made about how to do this.
- Then read through the advice on what is required and mark your own answer. Did you interpret the question successfully? Read through the answers given and note where the marks were awarded. Finally, read through the comments to see what a full answer should include. If using a different option application, use the skills that are discussed and apply the ideas to your own answer.
- Once you have prepared answers for all the questions in a particular area, answer them again, but this time choose a different focus/different material. For example, if you described one explanation of schizophrenia, perhaps the neurotransmitter explanation, describe another explanation, perhaps the other biological one you learned or the non-biological one. If the question is about one in-depth area (e.g. the DSM-IV-TR or DSM-5 classification), answer it as if it were about the other in-depth area (e.g. the ICD). In this way you are making up your own questions, which is useful preparation for the examination.
- Specimen assessment materials can be found on the Edexcel website (www.edexcel.com), together with mark schemes. When you think you have revised enough, look them up and try to answer the questions. You may need your teacher to help you to access these materials.

■ Clinical psychology

Overview

(1) Describe what is meant by clinical psychology. (3 marks)

ⓔ There are 3 points-based AO1 marks. There is 1 mark for each point that focuses on what clinical psychology is. For a 'describe' injunction, aim to develop points a little. **Note:** you could use the same question for any of the topic areas, such as your option application, to change this question.

Student answer

Clinical psychology is about explaining mental health issues and focusing on ways of treating them. Diagnosis is important, so that treatment can be suggested to suit the diagnosis so issues like reliability of diagnosis are also important. If two or more clinicians diagnosing the same person do not come up with the same diagnosis, the diagnosis is unreliable and different courses for the mental disorder might then be suggested as well as different treatments. ✔ Clinical psychologists are guided by NICE about what treatments are suitable for specific disorders, such as CBT being evidence-based and recommended for mental disorders like unipolar depression. ✔ Treatment choice clearly relies on diagnosis. Mental disorders can be explained referring to biology and genes or referring to environmental triggers, or both. Diagnoses come with explanations, such as schizophrenia being diagnosed if someone is experiencing hallucinations, with other features and symptoms too, and the explanation being related to neurotransmitter functioning. ✔ Diagnosis, explanation and treatment tend to go together in clinical psychology. If a disorder is explained by referring to neurotransmitter functioning, drug treatment might be seen as appropriate.(✔)

ⓔ **3/3 marks awarded.** There is enough here for 4 marks as shown by the tick in brackets. There is quite a lot of information about what clinical psychology includes in your course. In fact the answer is packed with information rather than being focused on clinical psychology in general. However, there is focus on the overall job of the clinical psychologist and the three areas of diagnoses, explanations and treatments are all covered. Although the answer is perhaps not that well focused, in a 'describe' answer it is the content that is needed, with no justification or discussion, so it gets full marks.

Content

(1) Define the four terms that are the four 'D's of diagnosis: danger, distress, dysfunction and deviance. (4 marks)

ⓔ There are 4 points-based AO1 marks. There is 1 mark for each definition. Be ready to define terms for 2 marks, though just 1 mark is allocated for each term here. **Note:** you could use any term or terms from this and/or your option application to change this question.

Student answer

Danger refers to violent behaviour directed towards others, which means danger for others, or behaviour that is a danger to the individual such as suicidal thoughts. ✔ *Distress* refers to the negative feelings that someone with a mental disorder tends to experience and links to the idea that abnormality, which means not fitting in with society's norms, brings with it negative emotions. ✔ *Dysfunction* is defined as someone not successfully carrying out everyday tasks and not living their life as they might have expected, with their behaviour not being successful and not working for them. ✔ *Deviance* refers to behaviour and feelings that are not the usual ones found in a society so they go against social norms and also these behaviours and feelings are not accepted by society. ✔

e **4/4 marks awarded.** All four terms are identified and it is clear what each means in relation to a person with a mental disorder, so each gets the 1 definition mark. The answer shows how the terms relate to a diagnosis of mental disorder, although the question just asks for the terms to be defined. If you needed to add more, such as if there were 2 marks for each definition, you could think about using an example, to show knowledge with understanding.

(2) Explain two strengths of the neurotransmitter explanation of schizophrenia.   (4 marks)

e There are 4 points-based AO3 marks. With two strengths required, this means 2 + 2 marks (2 marks for each strength). 'Explain' requires you to make a point and then justify it, so do that for each strength. **Note:** you could use a different explanation, a different disorder and/or weaknesses rather than strengths to change this question.

Student answer

Two neurotransmitter explanations for schizophrenia are the glutamate hypothesis and the dopamine hypothesis. One strength is that the glutamate and dopamine hypotheses don't contradict one another because the two are part of the neurotransmitter explanation of schizophrenia. ✔ Another strength is that evidence for the glutamate and dopamine hypotheses comes from neuroimaging which can be shown to be reliable because different people can separately analyse scans and if they come up with the same results that shows reliability. ✔

e **2/4 marks awarded.** There is a lot here but not quite enough in each case for the second mark. The first point about the two hypotheses working together needs evidence to justify it, such as adding: 'According to Carlsson et al. (2000), excess dopamine leads to psychosis-like symptoms and relates to schizophrenia. They also show that there is more to it. NDMA antagonists lead to psychosis-like symptoms and inhibit dopamine release. Carlsson et al. (2000) show that glutamate and dopamine are both involved and evidence like this strengthens the explanation.' The second point almost gets the 2 marks. There is some elaboration regarding how reliability of scanning can be tested and this nearly gives the second mark. However, some evidence would be useful, such as: 'Scanning shows that if people with schizophrenia are given amphetamines there is more release of dopamine than in those without schizophrenia, suggesting sensitivity to having excess dopamine. Using scanning to "see" the excess dopamine can be replicated.'

(3) Sabrina has been diagnosed with unipolar depression and has been prescribed a biological treatment by Roman, her GP. Sabrina wants to know more about the treatment. Explain to Sabrina one biological treatment that Roman could have suggested. You must make reference to the context in your answer.

(4 marks)

ⓔ There are 4 points-based AO2 marks. 'Explain' requires you to make a point and then justify it, so do that for each point you make about a biological treatment for Sabrina relating to her unipolar depression. You could describe a point about the treatment and explain it 'to Sabrina', which would be justifying the point. You know these are AO2 marks because you are asked to refer to the context. **Note:** you could use a different treatment and/or a different mental disorder to change the question.

Student answer

Roman could have suggested drug therapy such as antidepressants, which affect neurotransmitter functioning. He could explain to Sabrina that the idea is that neurotransmitter functioning, such as through a lack of serotonin, causes the depression. Neurotransmitters are chemicals used in the brain to pass messages and messages include thoughts and emotions. ✔ Changing neurotransmitter functioning, such as increasing serotonin at the synapse, would improve the depression. ✔ Sabrina needs to know how chemicals work at the synapse and what it is. It could be explained that there are gaps between brain cells and chemicals cross the gap to pass on a message. SSRIs increase serotonin by preventing its reuptake at the synapse and reuptake means taking serotonin back into the brain cells. ✔ By taking it back, that decreases the serotonin available and serotonin is lowered and so not available to pass on messages between brain cells. This links to depression and allowing more serotonin means less depressive thinking and fewer sad emotions. ✔

ⓔ **4/4 marks awarded.** There is a lot here, enough for all the marks, though it is not easy (or necessary) to see where the ticks go. They are inserted here to show likely places. The answer names a drug therapy, which is a biological treatment, though better to say what SSRI stands for. Then how the therapy works is explained. It is explained in 'layman' terms as well, as it needs to be explained to Sabrina. The answer describes how SSRIs work, which is not in the question, but there is enough here that is repeated in normal terms and focused on 'talking' to someone about their treatment to justify the description points, so the 'explain' injunction is responded to. In an AO2 question like this, about a context, avoid pure description (which would be AO1).

Methods (useful for Paper 3 as well as Paper 2)

(1) Using research, evaluate the case study research method for researching mental disorders.

(8 marks)

ⓔ There are 8 levels-based marks: 4 AO1 marks and 4 AO3 marks. You do not have to describe the case study method. The 4 AO1 marks will be inferred from your answer if you do not describe directly, as is shown in this student answer. 'Evaluate' requires you to come to a conclusion and 'supported judgement'. You need to look at the case study research method and your course asks you to know one study using the method, so draw on that too as the question says 'using research'. Focus on evaluating, which means drawing on evidence including strengths and weaknesses.

Student answer

The case study research method involves an in-depth and detailed study of one unique individual or a small group and is often used at an exploratory level, to look for results that can then be tested perhaps experimentally. There is an idiographic focus, which means the individual's mental disorder is what is important, rather than a nomothetic approach, which is about uncovering universal laws. Experiments and other methods gathering quantitative data are more likely to look for universal laws about behaviour and disorders. Case studies can gather some quantitative data, as they tend to involve many methods. However, there is a strong emphasis on qualitative data.

One example is Lavarenne et al. (2013), who carried out a case study of a small group (the Thursday group) which supports patients with psychosis and the research showed that one function of the group was to support the patients' fragile ego boundaries. The group acted as a boundary for individual members, where they could affirm their individual status and be heard. The data were qualitative, being the stories of the group gathered in one session. An advantage of the case study method is that data are valid. Lavarenne et al. (2013) noted down what happened in that one group session, which meant describing the stories of the patients who attended. This was a real group that was not put together for research purposes, which gives it ecological validity. Experiments or surveys used to gather data regarding mental health issues tend to be artificial, so not so valid.

A problem with case studies, however, is reliability. For example, Lavarenne et al. (2013), though they could repeat the study with the same group on a different day, which helps with reliability, could not repeat the exact study and so findings might not be consistent. There could be something about that particular meeting that was unique and there could be something about that group of patients or the therapists that was unique, which means limited reliability. In fact as case studies look at unique situations reliability is probably hard to establish. Generalisability is difficult as well, again because of the uniqueness of the individual or small group, setting and interaction being studied. For example, one of the stories given in Lavarenne et al. (2013), which involved an individual's history with the OPEC pipeline, was unique so valid but possibly not generalisable or reliable.

In conclusion, it seems that a strength of case studies is that they tend to be valid because of the reality of the situation and person/people being studied. However, they tend not to be easy to test for reliability because they are not inherently replicable. They tend not to be generalisable because of the uniqueness of the sample, so saying the findings are true for all of the target population (such as all with psychosis) is not possible. Also they take an idiographic and not a nomothetic view so drawing up universal laws about mental disorders is not what they enable. They gather qualitative, rich, in-depth data from unique real situations, which is their strength. They lack reliability, generalisability and the ability to draw up general laws of behaviour from them, which is their weakness.

(e) **6/8 or 7/8 marks awarded.** Q3, A-level Paper 1 in the Edexcel sample assessment materials shows the mark scheme for an 8-mark 'evaluate' question (page 32). There are no ticks in this student answer because it is marked according to quality and levels, not quantity. For full marks you need to show accurate and thorough knowledge with understanding (AO1), show well-developed logical evaluation with logical chains of reasoning throughout, use competing arguments and make a balanced conclusion. This answer does those things well. There is a lot of knowledge with understanding shown when the detail of Lavarenne et al. (2013) is included. What helps here is the use of detail such as the name of the group (Thursday group) and the reference to the OPEC pipeline, as well as detail about the case study method itself. Perhaps a bit more about the method would be better, such as which methods are usually put together and which methods were used in Lavarenne et al. (2013). Perhaps not 'thorough' — just into Level 4, but close to Level 3. With regard to the evaluation part, the use of the terms helps, such as validity, reliability and generalisability. Some points about interpretation and possible subjectivity would be useful as well. Use of the terms 'idiographic' and 'nomothetic', which are not part of the course but add depth to this evaluation, is good, though you can get full marks without going outside it. The conclusion summarises the competing arguments but could have picked up on the exploratory nature of case studies. Level 3/4, perhaps room for a bit more balance and logic in the argument.

Studies

(1) Describe two of Rosenhan's (1973) results. (2 marks)

(e) There are 2 points-based AO1 marks. Give two results from Rosenhan's (1973) study in reasonable detail so that you show knowledge with understanding. This is pure recall, you just need to 'describe'. **Note:** you could use this question for any study you have covered.

Student answer

Rosenhan's (1973) study was called 'On Being Sane in Insane Places', which explains the results. He found that when someone presented at a hospital saying they heard 'thud' or something similar in their head, which is just one symptom of schizophrenia, they were admitted into the hospital and only released (most were diagnosed with 'schizophrenia in remission') after quite a few days (19 days on average). ✔ Another result was in another part of the study where people working in a hospital were told there might be some pseudo-patients arriving when this was not planned. 41 'patients' were identified by at least one member of staff to be pseudo-patients when, as far as Rosenhan knew, there was none. ✔ This showed that diagnosing schizophrenia is very hard to do and not valid.

🄮 **2/2 marks awarded.** This answer clearly gives detail about the findings. There is more detail than just the two results, as there is a conclusion at the end and the introductory sentence does not give results. However, the two main results are given and there is detail, such as the average number of days before the pseudo-patients got home. Note that in this section, good detail is asked for before a mark is given — you are likely to need to write quite a bit for each mark.

(2) Explain two differences between Rosenhan (1973) and Carlsson et al. (2000) in terms of their research method. (4 marks)

🄮 There are 4 points-based AO3 marks. With 4 marks and two things to do (two differences in this case), this means 2 + 2 in the marking (each difference has 2 marks). **Note:** you could use similarities instead of differences, or practical uses, to change the question, or you could use two different studies or one of these and one other study.

Student answer

One difference between Rosenhan's and Carlsson et al.'s research methods is that they have a very different focus. Rosenhan (1973) uses a case study method in that it is an in-depth look at one area, but there are elements of a field experiment because the 'hearing thud' is set up, different participants are used, and eight hospitals, so it is not a case study as such. Carlsson et al. (2000) use biological methods including animal experiments and neuroimaging to look at brain functioning. The difference is that one is looking at how schizophrenia is diagnosed and at validity of diagnosis whereas the other is looking at how schizophrenia can be explained, looking at neurotransmitters, and it is this focus that gave the different research methods chosen. ✔✔ Another difference is that Carlsson et al. (2000) uses animal experiments to give evidence for a glutamate hypothesis to explain schizophrenia, alongside dopamine issues, whereas Rosenhan (1973) sticks to humans and individuals who answer all questions truthfully, giving validity, even though the one main issue (what they hear in their heads) is not true. What is found from humans is surely more valid and generalisable than what is found from animal studies, which is a main difference. ✔✔

🄮 **4/4 marks awarded.** There is a lot of material in this answer and it seems to take some time to make each 'difference' point but in the end they are made and are clear. It would be better perhaps to give the difference first and then the justification for the point as the marker has to track back to find the justification. Each of the two difference points could be made more simply. For example, using animals or humans is a research method difference. It would be clearer to state this without mentioning validity, even if generalisability is then brought in. However, there is enough here for the full marks. What is good is that the question is answered — the research methods are compared using differences.

Key question

> Employees with mental health issues like depression, anxiety and schizophrenia might think they need to stop working. However, an article on the 'time to change' website urges such people to get support. A strong message is that they are not alone and have rights, support is out there.

(1) **Discuss, using concepts, theories and/or research in clinical psychology, the key question for society of the issues surrounding mental health in the workplace. You must make reference to the context in your answer.**
(8 marks)

ⓔ There are 8 levels-based marks: 4 AO1 marks (knowledge and understanding) and 4 AO2 marks (applying psychology to the source/key question). 'Discuss' asks you to explore the issue, giving different viewpoints. You do not have to come to a conclusion or judgement. Page 111 of the Edexcel A-level sample assessment materials has a levels mark scheme for an 8-mark 'discuss' question with stimulus material, which is the mark scheme that would be used for this question. You need to draw on material you have learned in clinical psychology to talk about mental health in the workplace. **Note:** you can use the internet to look up a brief source about your own key question to use as the stimulus material and then insert the 'new' key question into this one to change the question.

Student answer

Mental disorders can be diagnosed using issues such as danger, distress, dysfunction and deviance. **AO1** If someone poses a danger to others perhaps that is an issue for employers. Although a lot of mental disorders pose little problem to other individuals, such as anxiety and depression, there might be an issue with side effects of medication, such as dizziness and fatigue that can come from, for example, SSRIs. **AO1** Such side effects might be an issue for employers and need to be reported perhaps. The WHO Report (2005) suggests amitriptyline is not so well tolerated as other tricyclics and SSRIs, **AO1** so it can depend what medication someone is on. The source suggests employees need to take a positive view and don't have to give up work, though an employer might need to be reassured about danger to the individual and to others.

However, on a more positive note, if someone is 'not alone' in having a mental disorder diagnosis like anxiety and depression, which are relatively common, that might help employees to have the confidence to ask employers for help rather than being stigmatised, as the source suggests. In the USA around 6.7% of adults can suffer from depression at any one time, and in the UK from 2010 to 2011 depression affected over 4.7 million people. **AO1** If something like depression or anxiety is common then it might not be seen as deviant behaviour in a society and stigma should be lifted with consequences for how people with mental disorders feel in the workplace. As the source says, they do not need to stop working.

Distress in the individual can be treated, which again should mean someone can stay in work. CBT is an evidence-based treatment for anxiety and depression and can help with schizophrenia as well as phobias, OCD and anorexia nervosa. **AO1** CBT involves someone examining their thinking and how it drives their emotions and their behaviour. If someone has a phobia their thoughts are going to be negative about encountering their phobia. Thinking about such an encounter makes them anxious and fearful, which probably means they avoid the situation. The consequences are that they do not discover they will be okay and the fearful thought about the situation remains. **AO1** If a phobia links to work, the person might need help in sticking with their fears to get rid of the phobia, and if employers can give some support that can help as this sort of treatment can be successful. Kuyken et al. (2008) reported that a group-based form of CBT, which is called 'mindfulness-based cognitive therapy', was as good at treating depression as drugs like Prozac and better at preventing relapse, as well as being cost-effective. **AO1** NICE guidelines recommend CBT for a lot of mental disorders and employers could help by providing space and time for such therapy. The source suggests employees ask for help in this sort of way.

Brown (1986) carried out a study looking at depression in women and found that of those who had no support 44% developed depression. **AO1** This suggests support at work is very important and social support helps those with schizophrenia as well. Not only does this suggest that there needs to be support in the workplace to avoid developing depression, it suggests that employers and others being supportive at work can act as a therapy in itself. This helps society as it is cost-effective both in terms of not having to offer therapy to someone with mental health issues and in terms of being cost-effective in industry in terms of production and fewer lost days of work.

ⓔ Around 6/8 marks awarded. There is accurate and thorough knowledge and understanding, given the time available for a question like this (perhaps around 12 minutes). **AO1** at the end of a sentence or piece of writing in this answer indicates knowledge and understanding to help you to see where this applies. The answer is well balanced as it looks at quite a few concepts, theories and studies, as shown by **AO1**. Kuyken et al. (2008) is a study that suits this key question, as is Brown (1986). There is some awareness of competing arguments around the discussion of how an employer has to be mindful of any danger both for the individual and for others, compared with the argument that there are a lot of mental health issues, it is common and needs to be supported by employers. The answer looks at how treatment can help and employers should make provision for treatment, such as CBT. There is relevant evidence, such as side effects of SSRIs and mention of other tricyclics. The source is referred to, both looking at the support that should be asked for and the comment about those with mental disorders in the workplace not being alone. Alongside the accurate and reasonably thorough knowledge and understanding shown, there is some logical and balanced discussion with some chains of reasoning, though there is a tendency to present points separately. Overall this answer is very close to the top level (7 or 8 marks) but needs to be a bit more organised with some more detail (such as evidence for the effectiveness of CBT).

Practical investigation

(1) As part of your study of clinical psychology you will have carried out a summative content analysis, probably including the Chi-squared test.

> **(a)** Give two of the categories you used in your summative content analysis. (2 marks)

ℯ There are 2 points-based AO1 marks. You need to show what you used as categories or themes in the content analysis. Give only two. 'Give' is like 'state', and is measuring recall. **Note:** you could try giving four categories if you had more than two, or you could change the question to asking about two stages you used in your content analysis.

> **Student answer**
>
> I used stigma ✔ as one (negative) category and acceptance ✔ as another (positive) category and I used others as well.

ℯ **2/2 marks awarded.** The practical in clinical psychology has to focus on attitudes towards mental health so the answer has to give two categories that can be attitudes to mental health. You are just asked to 'give' two categories, you do not need to describe or explain, for example. There is a stigma around mental disorder perhaps, and there can be acceptance, so these two are fine.

> **(b)** Explain one strength and one limitation of your content analysis. (4 marks)

ℯ There are 4 points-based AO3 marks. 4 marks and two things to do means 2 + 2 in the marking. Give one good point in your own content analysis and justify your point. Then give one weakness of your own content analysis and justify your point. The question is not asking for strengths and limitations of content analysis as a research method but of your own practical investigation using content analysis. You are not asked to evaluate your content analysis directly. However, as you had to conduct a content analysis you would be expected to know one thing you did well and one limitation with what you did. **Note:** you could use two strengths or two limitations to change the question.

> **Student answer**
>
> One thing I did well in my content analysis was to use one each of a 'broadsheet' and 'red top' and two editions of each to get a variety of views. I read through the whole of each paper slowly to look for any reference to mental disorder, not just headings, so what I did well was to be thorough and look for different views.

ℯ **2/4 marks awarded.** This answer gives one strength of the student's practical investigation with detail that would be expected to show in practice what the strength was. However, there is no limitation. A limitation might be that there were just the two different 'brands' of newspaper and just two editions of each, so although this seemed like 'variety' in practice it was perhaps a rather limited sample. The fact that it was in only one country, presumably, could also be mentioned when discussing limitation of the sample.

Issues and debates (Papers 1, 2 and 3)

(1) To what extent does clinical psychology reflect psychology as science?　　　　(20 marks)

Ⓒ There are 20 marks: 8 AO1 marks for knowledge and understanding, which can be inferred from your answer or which you can write as separate points, and 12 AO3 marks for evaluation and argument. 'To what extent' involves bringing in a balanced and reasoned argument, then bringing points together to form a judgement or conclusion. You need to show you understand what 'psychology as science' means and throughout bring in examples from clinical psychology to illustrate 'science' and also examples showing 'not science'. **Note:** you can use this question for any of the applications or you could use a different 'issue and debate' to discuss, in order to change the question.

Student answer

Clinical psychology is about mental disorders, which are diagnosed using the DSM or the ICD, which involve lists of symptoms and features. Diagnosis by matching such symptoms to a 'disorder' already shows clinical psychology to be scientific in that there is not meant to be interpretation by the clinician regarding which diagnosis to choose. Science involves objectivity and 'facts', which are measured empirically and can be found again as they have to be reliable. A diagnosis by one clinician has to match one of the same person by another clinician to show reliability, otherwise it is not worth much, it is an individual opinion. An individual opinion does not help in deciding treatment or in conveying to society the issues a person has, to help with them getting funds or helping their workplace to understand.

Science according to Popper involves having a theory, generating one or more hypotheses from it, testing the ideas against reality and then either accepting the hypothesis to support the theory, amending the theory or rejecting the theory. According to Popper the idea should be to falsify the theory as proving it is not possible, though in psychology hypotheses tend to make statements about what a theory would predict rather than about falsifying it. To make sure that it is just the expectation in the hypothesis that is tested, there should be no subjectivity from a researcher and there must be reliability and objectivity to find results that show cause-and-effect conclusions.

In order to 'be scientific' in this way, psychology tends to opt for experiments, which can show the required controls, manipulate just one variable of interest, which is the independent variable, and measure the resulting change in the dependent variable. One way to justify an application for its element of science is to consider the research methods used, to see if they can show reliability and objectivity. Science is also about the subject matter tested, because that has to be testable scientifically. It has to be possible to measure empirically what is to be studied. Another way to see if an application is scientific is to see if its subject matter is testable scientifically and whether there is strong theory from which to derive a hypothesis that can have operationalised variables that can be measured empirically.

To see if clinical psychology reflects psychology as science, first its subject matter is considered and then the methods it uses are looked at. In both cases the idea of clinical psychology being 'science' is considered as well as it being 'not science' before a conclusion is drawn.

Clinical psychology looks at treatment for mental disorders including drug therapy and it also considers explanations for such disorders including genes and neurotransmitter functioning. Biology is a science and clinical psychology draws on science so it is a science to that extent. However, treatment can also include CBT, which is about thoughts and emotions, not subject matter that is easily measurable. Mindfulness can be used, which is about putting the past and future to one side and thinking about the present. This is about feelings and emotions, as is depression and anxiety, both topics in clinical psychology, so not all of clinical psychology is 'science'. Carlsson et al. (2000) is a scientific study about schizophrenia using animal studies and studies using scanning to find out about dopamine and glutamate functioning in the brain. However, Rosenhan (1973) sent individuals into hospitals just being themselves but saying they heard things like 'thud' in their heads to see what was going on in such hospitals and what a diagnosis of schizophrenia was like, which is not a scientifically careful measure, but an holistic approach involving how the people felt.

Clinical psychology uses animal experiments and neuroimaging to find out about how the brain works, including neurotransmitter functioning as an explanation for schizophrenia and including drug therapy relating to such functioning as a treatment for schizophrenia. Animal experiments use many controls so that only the independent variable is manipulated, such as lesioning in a certain brain area to look at how dopamine receptors are affected, such as in schizophrenia seeing how supersensitivity to dopamine can work in animals. Brain scanning also shows dopamine linking to schizophrenia, such as when people are given amphetamines there is more dopamine released in people with schizophrenia than in those who do not have schizophrenia. Scanning gives pictures that can be assessed by more than one person and scans can be repeated so reliability can be checked. Objectivity can be shown if the person analysing the scans is not 'in on' the hypothesis. Scanning and animal experiments are 'scientific' and this shows a large element of science in clinical psychology's methods.

However, clinical psychology also uses studies of humans and it is hard to be 'scientific' when researching, for example, schizophrenia in humans. Pihlajamaa et al. (2008) used the case notes of 807 people in Finland and compared the diagnosis using the ICD-10 and the DSM-III-R or DSM-IV to see if different diagnostic systems came up with the same diagnosis. It was validity that was looked for. The same diagnosis was found about 75% of the time for the ICD-10 and the DSM so they matched for validity. Using case notes has validity, because they are about 'real' people. However, the data are not that scientific. The researchers could only use people who had diagnosis from at least two systems and the findings were true only of those in Finland. This is in a way empirical data as case notes were used. However, 'diagnosis' does not give sense data (empirical data) but will include some interpretation by a clinician even though it is not meant to. It is not the same as damaging an animal's brain region and drawing conclusions from the resulting behaviour about what the region is for. Science should not include interpretation and as 'diagnosis' is not easily empirically measurable (individuals make the decisions), there is an element of clinical psychology not being science.

Clinical psychology also relies on case study evidence as Lavarenne et al. (2013) show. They make careful notes about one session of a support group for people with schizophrenia to show that the group helped to give the individuals boundaries they, as individuals with schizophrenia and psychosis, were struggling with. In-depth and detailed valid data are obtained by case studies but what is noted down is chosen, which leads to an element of subjectivity, and one specific group session is not replicable so reliability is hard to show. Case studies focus on validity and are not 'scientific' to the extent that objectivity and reliability are missing, and what is being measured is not empirically testable.

In conclusion, it seems that clinical psychology looks at scientific subject matter that is in many ways empirically testable using reliable and objective measuring. This includes neurotransmitters and the function of certain brain regions and using methods like animal experiments and brain scanning. However, clinical psychology also looks at thoughts and feelings, using CBT as a therapy, for example, and mindfulness. It looks at how valid diagnoses are and how people with schizophrenia are treated in hospital. It uses case study evidence and examines case files in areas where interpretation and subjectivity are involved in analysis. A judgement might be that clinical psychology is to a great extent scientific in order to draw cause-and-effect conclusions about individuals and their treatment and care. However, there is another large element of clinical psychology that is about people's feelings and the care of individuals that is not scientific.

@ **17/20 marks awarded (Level 4).** The top level for this type of question will ask for accurate and thorough knowledge and understanding. There is a lot of knowledge and understanding here, about what science is, methods in psychology and features of clinical psychology. The answer is thorough in that studies and evidence are brought in, and it is accurate, so it gains Level 4 for that part of the answer. With regard to the AO3 element, lines of argument are supported by evidence in the main, though a named animal study perhaps would be useful. Each of the points of development has some evidence for the claim made. There is some integrating too in that after the first paragraph giving some ideas, the next shows what science is and thereafter points relate back to whether they are about science as defined, or not. The answer does draw together ideas that show development and so responds to the question. There is some planning, showing the reader that the answer is about the material in clinical psychology as well as research methods, and paragraphing follows this thread. There is a conclusion and a judgement at the end that draws on the material presented. What is needed is a well-developed and logical evaluation with chains of reasoning, which is perhaps not quite there. There is an awareness of competing arguments (science and not science) and a balanced response with a balanced conclusion. In the time available, this is a thorough answer and scores a high mark.

■ Option applications: criminological, child and health psychology

Overview

(1) Describe one feature that defines criminological psychology. (2 marks)

ⓔ There are 2 points-based AO1 marks. This question is asking you to choose one feature that would tell someone what criminological psychology is. Say what that feature is and then develop the answer. You do not need to give a justification of your point. One way of developing a point is to use an example, but give enough in the example to show understanding. This question is within criminological psychology. **Note:** if you are studying child or health psychology you can still use this question, or you can focus on two features to change the question.

> **Student answer**
>
> One feature of criminological psychology that defines it is the treatment of offenders by forensic psychologists, focusing on assessment of needs, formulation using theory to decide on a treatment plan, and then carrying out the treatment, which might be, for example, anger management or CBT. ✔✔

ⓔ **2/2 marks awarded.** This answer clearly gives one feature. You can find features in the specification at the start of the application (also for child and health psychology) and 'treatment' is one of them for criminological psychology. The development of the answer to show understanding of the stages that are gone through when setting up and carrying out treatment is useful. Giving examples of treatments alone would not be enough. Leaving out the bit of the answer 'focusing on assessment ... carrying out the treatment' would mean 1 mark and not 2 marks.

Content

(1) What is meant by attachment and privation in child psychology? (2 marks)

ⓔ There are 2 points-based AO1 marks, with 1 mark for each definition. This question is within child psychology. **Note:** you can pick out two terms from criminological or health psychology to change the question, or change the terms in child psychology.

> **Student answer**
>
> Attachment refers to an emotional bond initially formed between the caregiver and an infant or child, and continuing into adulthood, connecting two people in a deep and enduring way. ✔ Privation refers to the lack of an attachment forming and differs from deprivation because no emotional bond has formed at all, there not having been one for it to be broken. ✔

ⓔ 2/2 marks awarded. There is enough in each case for the 1 mark and the understanding of the two terms is clear. An example can help to elaborate to be sure of a mark, so it might be worth adding one, though as each term has just 1 mark you do not need to go into more detail. Note that there is quite a bit of detail here. Any point in an exam has to be made clearly and effectively to get a mark.

(2) Sai is telling his family about his treatment for his heroin addiction but cannot remember what he was told about it.

From a health psychologist's viewpoint, explain one treatment for heroin addiction to Sai and his family, to see if that is the treatment he has been offered. You must make reference to the context in your answer. (4 marks)

ⓔ There are 4 points-based marks. You know that this is an AO2 question because there is stimulus material and you are reminded to refer to the context in your answer. You should do that throughout the answer, not just once. You are asked to 'explain', which means making points and justifying them. For 4 marks you could make two clear points and justify them. **Note:** you can pick out one treatment from criminological or health psychology to change the question to suit your application, or change this question to comparing two treatments, for example, in health psychology.

Student answer

One treatment a health psychologist might explain to Sai and his family is drug therapy. Drugs used are methadone, buprenorphine and naltrexone, so he might have been prescribed one of these. It is likely that neither Sai nor the family will understand drug therapy fully so the health psychologist would explain what it is about in layman's terms. The psychologist would say that a substitute for heroin could be prescribed, which works in the same way, such as methadone, ✔ which they have probably heard of, being a synthetic opiate that mimics how heroin works in the brain and takes away withdrawal symptoms for about 24 hours. Methadone is like heroin in the brain so doing a similar job but without the withdrawal symptoms, which means it helps someone to come off heroin. ✔ Drugs for heroin addiction can be opioid receptor antagonists, though methadone is an opioid agonist and buprenorphine is a partial agonist. Antagonists block the effects of heroin and agonists mimic the heroin. Blocking means using a drug that does not suit the brain in the way heroin suits and so the signal that heroin would send is not sent. Drug treatment is about not getting the high, but not getting the withdrawal symptoms either. ✔ Sai might have been told he was having pharmacological treatment or medication so it would be worth mentioning these terms in case Sai remembers them. Of course there are other treatments such as CBT, which might have been recommended for Sai. The family might need to know that drug therapy like the use of methadone is given once a day and the addict has to go to a clinic to get the drug so it is an intensive treatment and Sai might need support with staying on the programme. ✔

ⓔ 4/4 marks awarded. There is a lot of information here and it is clearly focused on giving information to Sai and his family that would help him to stick with the treatment and to understand it. One treatment is focused on, which suits the question. More could be explained about agonists and antagonists as that part is not that clear, but it is good to show use of such terms and some understanding as well as naming three drugs. The factual information about methadone programmes, such as going to a clinic daily, would be helpful for the family. The answer is applying knowledge of a treatment to a situation, which is AO2, and that is what is being tested. The ticks are given where there is application of knowledge and understanding more than when there is AO1 description, as this question focuses on AO2.

Methods (also useful for Paper 3)

(1) Sofia and two colleagues wanted to look at the effects of pre-trial publicity on jury decision-making. They used a mock juror study using students from their university. The students had agreed as part of their course to take part in a specified number of psychology studies. Half of the students were shown newspaper cuttings writing negatively about the defendant in a trial that had happened 5 years before and the other half read newspaper cuttings about a by-election also given years before. Then the students were shown a video of the 5-year-old trial, showing the opening statements of the prosecution and the opening statements of the defence. The task was for the mock jurors to rate the guilt of the defendant in the trial on a scale of 1 (not guilty) to 7 (definitely guilty). Sofia and her colleagues thought that those who had seen negative pre-trial publicity would rate the defendant as more guilty than those who had read other material before seeing the trial video.

(a) State an experimental hypothesis for Sofia and her colleagues' study. (2 marks)

(e) There are 2 AO2 marks for giving a clear experimental hypothesis with the independent and the dependent variable operationalised. 'State' means 'give', which means show you understand what is required, showing knowledge of what an experimental hypothesis is, and what the IV and the DV and operationalising variables are. This question is within criminological psychology. **Note:** you could use a null hypothesis to change the question or you could use a brief summary of a study you covered in child or health psychology and write out the experimental or null hypothesis.

Student answer

There is a difference in the rating of guilt out of seven (1 = not guilty and 7 = definitely guilty) between the participants who read negative newspaper cuttings about the defendant in the trial they were shown using video compared with those who read about something unrelated to the crime (which was about a by-election). Those reading the pre-trial publicity would rate the defendant as more guilty than those reading about the by-election. ✔✔

(e) **2/2 marks awarded.** This answer clearly shows what the IV is (whether what is read beforehand is negative pre-trial publicity about the defendant or something else) and what the DV is (how guilty the participant rates the defendant after seeing the video of the trial opening statements). The experimental hypothesis should be directional, which the last sentence makes it, so that is good.

The results of Sofia's study are shown in the table below.

Table of results for the study, showing rating of guilty depending on whether participants read pre-trial publicity or were in the control condition (1 = not guilty and 7 – definitely guilty)

Participant	Read pre-trial publicity — rating of guilt	Participant	Read other material — rating of guilt
1	6	11	3
2	4	12	4
3	5	13	2
4	2	14	1
5	7	15	6
6	6	16	3
7	4	17	4
8	5	18	2
9	3	19	3
10	6	20	5

(b) What test would be needed for this study? Give three reasons why this test would be chosen. (2 marks)

ⓔ There are 2 points-based AO2 marks. You would get 1 mark for naming the test and one reason and 1 mark for the other two reasons. This question focuses on criminological psychology with regard to the source, but the question is a general one about methodology. **Note:** you could change this to a study using repeated measures to change the question (and the test), or you could change this to a study relating to child or health psychology to change the question to suit your application.

Student answer

The test is the Mann–Whitney U test. This is the test for looking for a difference ✔ when the data are ordinal (ranks) and it is an independent groups design. ✔

ⓔ **2/2 marks awarded.** The test is correct with three correct reasons so maximum marks. There is not much else you can say. You could say it is not a correlation but it is better to say it is a test of difference.

(c) (i) Carry out the test for Sofia's study, giving the test result. (1 mark)

ⓔ There is 1 points-based AO2 mark. This is AO2 because you are applying your understanding of which test to use and how to do the test. The workings are not required, though they might be required in an exam question. 1 mark is for the test result. **Note** you could change the data so that they relate to a repeated measures design, which would require a Wilcoxon test, to change the question.

Student answer

The test is a Mann–Whitney U test and the result is U = 24. ✔ (The total of ranks for List A is 131 and for List B is 79.)

ⓔ **1/1 mark awarded.** There is 1 mark for the right answer. This is just for the purposes of this Question & Answer section. In an exam you are likely to have to show the working and there would be more marks available. The workings shown here are to help you; there is no need to include them for the 1 mark available for this question. The formulae for the tests are in the specification and would be at the front of the exam papers. Practise doing the tests — they get easier with practice as they are then more familiar.

(c) (ii) Explain whether the test done in (b) (i) is significant at the
$p < 0.05$ level of significance. (2 marks)

ⓔ There are 2 points-based AO2 marks. They are AO2 because you are applying your understanding of how to check for significance. One of the marks would be for comparing the calculated value from (b) (i) and critical value in the table (which you can find in the specification) and the other for saying whether it is significant or not. This is about making the point about significance and then justifying the point, as it is an 'explain' injunction. **Note:** you can change the level of significance or whether the hypothesis needs to be one-tailed or two-tailed and/or the number of participants to change the question and practise using critical values tables.

> **Student answer**
>
> $U = 24$, there are 10 participants in each group, the hypothesis is directional (one-tailed) and the level of significance is $p < 0.05$. Using all this information the critical value is 27. ✔ For this test the calculated value must be equal to or less than the critical value, which it is (24 is less than 27), so the result is significant and the null hypothesis is rejected. ✔ The experimental hypothesis is accepted. Just to note that at $p < 0.01$ where the critical value is 19 the result would not be significant.

ⓔ **2/2 marks awarded.** There is 1 mark for the main point that the calculated value of 24 is less than the critical value of 27, as that is the information justification part of the answer. Then 1 mark for the point itself, which is that the result is significant and the null hypothesis is rejected. The answer does not need to add that the experimental hypothesis is accepted or to add that at $p < 0.01$ the result would not be significant, but it does show thorough understanding in adding this information.

(d) Explain one ethical issue with Sofia and her colleagues' study. (2 marks)

ⓔ There are 2 points-based AO3 marks. They are AO3 because although you need to consider ethical requirements when carrying out studies in psychology and then to apply your knowledge and understanding to the scenario/source, by considering ethics you are evaluating the study, and 'explain' means giving an ethical point and then justifying it. **Note:** you can change the question to include more than one ethical issue or you can use a different source study and apply this question to it, including using a study from child or health psychology if you wish.

Student answer

One ethical issue with using students from a university who have given consent to being participants in studies is that they do not give informed consent even though getting informed consent (usually in writing) from participants is part of the BPS *Code of Ethics and Conduct* (2009) within the principle 'respect'. ✔

ⓔ 1/2 marks awarded. This is a good answer with a lot of information, including bringing in the BPS code. However, to get the other mark a bit more about why the students' consent is not 'informed consent' would be needed. Perhaps explain more about the task, which is reading about pre-trial publicity which is negative and might be stressful, as well as having to watch the opening of a trial, also being stressful. The students did not consent to that.

Studies

(1) **Describe the aims of van Ijzendoorn and Kroonenberg (1988) and one study from Cassibba et al. (2013), Gagnon-Oosterwaal et al. (2012) or Li et al. (2013).** (4 marks)

ⓔ There are 4 points-based AO1 marks. The question focuses on the classic study in child psychology and one of three contemporary studies. You will have studied one of the contemporary studies named here. Be ready to pick out the study you chose, and not be put off by seeing named studies you may not know about. The aims are what the researchers set out to achieve. As there are 2 marks for each study's aims (which you would know from there being two things to do and an even number of marks), you need to write quite a bit in each case. This question focuses on child psychology. **Note:** you can choose to replace the question using the classic and contemporary studies from criminological or health psychology, and you can change the requirement for the aims, to ask about results or conclusions.

Student answer

van Ijzendoorn and Kroonenberg's (1988) meta-analysis aimed to see if Ainsworth's Strange Situation procedure used in different countries and cultures to look at attachment types had the same findings in the different countries. ✔ They wanted to look for a global distribution of child attachment types to see if bias is lessened by using a large sample of studies and if, for example, secure attachment is always found to be the most common attachment type. ✔ Cassibba et al. (2013) also used a meta-analysis and the team of researchers included van Ijzendoorn. Cassibba et al. (2013) also wanted to look at studies using the Strange Situation to see if attachment and the types Ainsworth uncovered were universal. ✔ They were very interested as well in 'attachment the Italian way' and for various reasons, such as the country being Catholic, they wondered whether attachment types in Italy differed from those in other countries. ✔

ⓔ **4/4 marks awarded.** This answer has a lot of information. Both studies have enough information about their aims to score the 2 marks. The question asked for description, so there was no need to compare the aims of the two studies. However, as their aims linked, by comparing them information was added to the description and was marked as development of the description.

Key question

(1) **Explain a key question for society using two concepts from health psychology.**   (6 marks)

ⓔ There are 6 points-based AO1 marks. They are AO1 marks, knowledge and understanding, as the question is asking about a key question you will have prepared. You may not have prepared using two concepts specifically. However, just choose two of the ones you have looked at. This question focuses on health psychology. **Note:** you can use criminological or child psychology instead and can vary the number of concepts to change the question.

> **Student answer**
>
> A key question in health psychology is how can people be encouraged to stop smoking. One idea is to consider the reward nicotine gives in the brain, which is reinforcing for an individual and would need to be replaced to help someone to stop smoking, otherwise they would want to continue with behaviour that is rewarded, following the principles of operant conditioning. ✔ One way a reward can be replaced is to consider financial rewards for quitting, however, another way is to use nicotine patches or another form of nicotine replacement therapy. Then the brain is getting nicotine via a different route and slowly the patches could be stopped so that the person was off nicotine altogether. ✔ Nicotine replacement therapy allows nicotine into the bloodstream more slowly, which still gives some pleasure but in a safer way such as avoiding harmful tar and also giving a weaker synapse response. ✔ Another concept is to focus on removing cues that are associated with the reward of a cigarette and nicotine. Cues can be in the place where someone usually smokes or the time, such as the end of a meal. ✔ If these cues or other cues for an individual are associated with smoking, then producing the cues without the smoking should help to extinguish the association. ✔ This is using principles of classical conditioning and is called cue-exposure therapy. Cue exposure and giving a different reward are two ways of encouraging stopping smoking in an individual.

ⓔ **5/6 marks awarded.** This answer is thorough enough and what is good about it is that it answers the question clearly, giving two different concepts (from operant and classical conditioning, and both therapies) and sticking with them. It is as much the structuring of the answer that gives it the high marks as it is that there is a lot of information. The missing mark is for the second concept, as although the additional part about classical conditioning is close to getting the mark, a bit more about conditioned stimulus and extinction, perhaps even mentioning spontaneous recovery, would add that bit to secure the final mark.

Practical investigation

(1) You will have carried out a practical investigation in criminological
psychology. Explain one way you could have improved your study.   (4 marks)

(e) There are 4 points-based AO3 marks. Expect questions that ask you to refine
procedures either in an unseen study given as stimulus material in the exam or
relating to your own or another study you have covered. This question is about
making one improvement to your study and there are 4 marks available so you
need to give a lot of information about your one improvement. This question is
within criminological psychology. **Note:** you can change the question to focus on
child or health psychology if you wish, or you can consider two problems and two
improvements with your practical investigation.

Student answer

In criminological psychology I carried out a laboratory experiment to look
at eyewitness memory. My participants watched a video of a man buying a
newspaper in a shop with the shopkeeper being rather aggressive to the man.
The participants were then asked questions about the video including the
important question that asked 'How aggressive was the shopkeeper?' or, in the
control condition, 'What was the shopkeeper's attitude like?' An improvement
would be using a field experiment with the shopkeeper being asked to behave
rather abruptly to some real customers over a few different days, focusing on
different customers. ✔ As a real shopkeeper might lose business that way,
a 'pop up' shop could be used in an empty shop with council permission. The
shopkeeper would be one of the researchers but the customers/participants
would be real. ✔ This would add ecological validity to the study, which would
be a field experiment not a laboratory experiment and would be carried out
in the customer's natural setting while the customer was shopping. ✔ After
the customer left the shop, another researcher could ask them four questions
about the scenario, to keep it short and not to take up too much of their time.
One of the questions could be 'What was the shopkeeper's attitude like?' and
the other 'How abrupt was the shopkeeper?' This keeps my study similar to the
lab experiment. I thought that when asked about how abrupt the shopkeeper
was I might get an answer such as 'a lot' so I gave a scale for the questions
using 1 as 'not abrupt' to 7 as 'very abrupt' and for the control question I left
the answer open for the participant to complete, so I could analyse for any
mention of abruptness. I did this for my lab study too, using 'aggression' instead.
'Aggression' seemed a bit strong for a real-life event. ✔

(e) **4/4 marks awarded.** The suggested solution is clear, it is using a field
experiment rather than a laboratory experiment, and the plan is quite sensible.
Perhaps using the scale for abruptness and no scale for the control condition
might be hard to make comparisons between the answers, but this is part of the
student's practical itself and not part of the improvement, so is not picked up on.
You can see that in the improvement ethics are considered. Always make ethical
suggestions in exams in your answers.

Clinical psychology

1 Nicotine disorder has danger involved for the individual because of health risks, and passive smoking is a health risk to others as well. There is dysfunction in smoking because it is not legal in many places now, including workplaces, so it can be an inconvenient 'habit'. It could also mean someone is not accepted for a job because of their smoking if it would affect their role. Campaigns against smoking are common and it can be distressing to think one is going against social norms or harming one's health. Smoking also costs a lot, which can be a distressing burden. Smoking now is against social norms and can be seen as deviant, although that was not always the case.

2 Kirk and Kutchins (1992) said that interviewers were not trained enough and the situation the interview took place in was often a research setting and not a real clinical setting, so validity was in doubt. Brown et al. (2001) used interviewing to show the reliability of diagnosis of anxiety disorder using the DSM-IV, so the criticism that the interviewing was not a reliable or valid measure might apply.

3 Predictive validity means what is found successfully predicts what happens in the future. For example, if conduct disorder is diagnosed in a child and they continue to behave disruptively over the years, that diagnosis has predictive validity (e.g. Kim-Cohen et al., 2005). Internal validity refers to experiments and means there are sufficient controls for there to be no confounding variables so the cause-and-effect conclusion drawn from an experiment has internal validity. This does not apply to evaluation of the validity of the DSM as experiments are not used to test the DSM. Ecological validity is about study findings relating to a real-life setting and situation and the criticism that interviews were done in a research environment and not in a clinical situation (Kirk and Kutchins, 1992) was about lack of ecological validity.

4 A symptom is about the health issue that characterises schizophrenia, such as hearing voices. A feature is also something that characterises schizophrenia but is not health-related, such as its incidence in the population (around 1%).

5 Neurotransmitters are released from the pre-synaptic terminal buttons into the synaptic gap. There, if they fit the receptors, they are taken up by the post-synaptic neuron. If a drug 'fits' but is not the neurotransmitter sending the message (e.g. not dopamine, such as an anti-schizophrenic drug) then this will 'block' the receptors so that the 'real' neurotransmitter is not 'taken up' and does not send the message.

6 Heritability means how much of a characteristic is down to genes and inherited. 64% means that 36% of that characteristic might come from environmental influences and 64% from what we inherit in the way of biological make-up and so on.

7 The social drift hypothesis suggests that those with schizophrenia drift down social levels rather than that social adversity is a cause of schizophrenia. With schizophrenia it is hard to hold down a job and to plan as well, so being in poverty and living alone with difficulties tends to come from schizophrenia.

8 The cognitive model focuses on thinking and information processing in the brain. As symptoms of unipolar depression are thoughts as well as moods, such as negative thinking and lack of interest as well as hopelessness, it seems sensible to suggest that it is cognition that is causing the depression. The cognitive triad is negative thinking about the self, the world and the future.

9 Belief modification is specific in schizophrenia because it is focusing on delusions and hallucinations, which are specific to schizophrenia. Also, accepting thinking rationally when it seems not to be rational is specific to schizophrenia.

10 Selective serotonin reuptake inhibitors (SSRIs) do what is said in their name. They focus on serotonin and block its reuptake into the pre-synaptic neuron. Reuptake means removing it from the synaptic gap. Blocking reuptake leaves serotonin in the gap to be taken up by the post-synaptic neuron, which means a message is sent. Low levels of serotonin characterise depression, so adding more serotonin works to alleviate depression.

11 Catastrophising means thinking and worrying about what might happen in the future. As this has not yet happened, it is not helpful to be anxious or depressed about it. Often, if not usually, the event that is worrying someone does not happen so it is better not to focus on it and to focus more on the here and now.

12 The Health and Care Professions Council (HCPC) regulates psychologists, sets out standards, and if a psychologist does not meet the standards they can be removed from the register, which means they cannot work as a 'clinical psychologist'.

13 Longitudinal designs use the same participants and track them over time whereas cross-sectional designs use different participants and gather data from them at the same moment in time.

14 Case studies and interviews both gather qualitative data, so that is a similarity. A difference is in the depth and detail. Interviewing can be part of a case study but it does not give the depth or richness of data that is required.

15 A strength is that there can be generalisation of the findings as 12 different hospitals were involved, with

one person going to each and producing the same findings.

16 RCTs involve randomising how participants are allocated to either a treatment or a waiting list control group and this means nothing separates the two groups except for the treatment. Cause-and-effect conclusions can be drawn that would not be possible without the control group giving the baseline measure (the situation without the treatment).

Criminological psychology

17 The four sampling techniques; the BPS *Code of Ethics and Conduct* (2009) and the data analysis section.

18 Other brain regions will be operating as well as the amygdala, such as prefrontal lobes being involved in decision-making. Taking one brain region and saying it 'causes' crime and antisocial behaviour is too simplistic when it comes to the brain's complexity.

19 The way the frontal lobes work to control impulses and plan behaviour, if affected negatively, might mean more aggression and lack of planning, which is a biological explanation of crime and antisocial behaviour. Someone might act in a criminal way and get labelled. The label is internalised by them and they feel they cannot change, so they carry on with the criminal behaviour and the prophecy is fulfilled. A social explanation is about how interactions between people affect behaviour; the biological explanation is about how our biological make-up affects behaviour.

20 $p < 0.0001$ means there is a less than one in 10,000 likelihood that the result was obtained by chance. This level of significance is more likely to show a Type II error than a Type I error because it is a very strict level.

21 If a witness's recall about an event is affected by a weapon being present, so their attention is on the weapon and other information is not recorded and so not recalled, that affects their testimony. They may not have attended to a perpetrator, for example, and so any identification of them in a line-up is suspect. Similarly, if questions after an event mislead the witness, such as asking them about a blue car when perhaps they have not noticed a blue car, then that can affect their testimony, which will not be accurate (about the car, for example). They may record that information as being present only after being asked about it, which makes their testimony unreliable. Police questioning can give post-event information and so can others who witnessed the situation if there is discussion between them after the event. Media articles may be read and may give post-event information. There is a lot of opportunity for unreliability in someone's testimony, which can lead to a miscarriage of justice.

22 Extraneous variables must be controlled for, such as participant and situational variables like noise and anxiety. Confounding variables are extraneous variables that were not controlled for and did affect the results.

23 Valentine and Mesout (2008) used people visiting the London Dungeon and asked them to take part in a study to look at their ability to identify a 'scary person' they encountered in the Dungeon. This was a volunteer sample. The people who volunteered to be part of the study were those in the sample.

24 Researchers: 1) Participants must be protected or people might stop agreeing to be studied if they hear about bad practice. 2) Participants must be protected or ill health might be the result, which society would then have to deal with, as well as it being harmful for the individual. 3) In practical terms, participants must be protected so that there is no stress from being a participant as their stress could affect the results, making them biased. Practising psychologists: (1) Clients and others need to trust a psychologist so there must be rules that engender trust, including a client being looked after. (2) In a profession such as forensic psychology, there is likely to be multi-agency working where practitioners from different fields work together. Psychologists must work with other practitioners in an open and transparent way working for the benefit of an offender and/or any victims. (3) Forensic psychologists might have to present a case formulation to a judge or might have to meet up with an offender's family. There need to be rules about such interactions to protect all parties.

25 'Smashed' gave 40.8 mph; 'collided' gave 39.3 mph; 'bumped' gave 38.1 mph; 'hit' gave 34.0 mph and 'contacted' gave 31.8 mph.

26 (1) Loftus has shown quite clearly that leading questions or misleading information can affect someone's memory and thus affect their witness statement. Those asked about a yield sign, when there was no yield sign, and those asked about broken glass when there was none, did tend to 'remember' what they were asked about. This suggests our memory is not like a tape recorder and is affected by what we are asked, so I would say witness testimony involving such questioning is unreliable. (2) When there is a weapon in the scene this affects people's ability to identify a perpetrator. This would lead me not to trust eyewitness identification.

Child psychology

27 Child psychology is about the development of the individual from birth to adolescence and on into older age and it is about issues such as how early experiences affect our later decisions and development.

28 Mother as a safe base; child showing separation anxiety; mother showing sensitive mothering.

29 Good quality care and a lot of stimulation are said to help when overcoming the effects of privation or deprivation (and another important point is to start such intervention early where possible).

30 (1) The type of day care makes a difference, for example full-time nursery care led to good cognitive and language development but more behavioural problems later. (2) The quality of care makes a difference, with good quality care — characterised by low adult-to-child ratios and good stimulation — being advantageous, but poor quality care being detrimental. (3) The length of time in day care per week makes a difference (and also the age of the child). More than 20 hours a week (and under one year old), for example, seem to be detrimental.

31 The UNCRC (1989) gives a child participation and protection rights and ethics suggest that using psychology as social control is not a moral or ethical thing to do. A therapy that rewards 'appropriate' behaviour where it appears that the child has no say in it is less ethical than one that works with the child to encourage them in behaviour that helps them to live a life that suits them. It is about making sure a child is given their rights according to the UNCRC, such as Article 12, where the child is given the right to express a view and for their view to be given weight.

32 (a) qualitative data; (b) quantitative data. The first, (a), is the open question.

33 A privated child like Genie (Curtiss, 1977) might find it hard to fully participate in research about them because of lack of understanding (e.g. of language and customs) and they would need to be protected from researching being done 'to' them.

34 Securely attached children are found 70% of the time according to Ainsworth's study and this is the US norm. The other 30% is split just about evenly between anxious avoidant and anxious resistant.

35 In Western culture (and presumably all cultures) it is assumed that parents want the best for their child. This is a cultural norm, if not about parental 'nature'. Society wants the best upbringing because a workforce that is educated and healthy is required. Parents want something similar possibly because of living in such a society. It is hard to say why a parent is very protective of their child. This is an interesting question. The attachment bond can be said to be two-way, which is one answer.

Health psychology

36 Withdrawal refers to symptoms (physical and psychological), such as dizziness and headaches, that come once a drug that someone is dependent upon is stopped. Tolerance refers to having to take more of a drug to get the same effect. The difference is that one is about the body getting used to the drug and there needing to be more, whereas the other is about the body coping without the drug and responding accordingly.

37 The action of drugs seems to be in the brain's reward pathways, even if also elsewhere, and the action

increases the amount of dopamine in the reward systems. Dopamine is what gives the pleasure response and if all drugs work on the pathways and mean there is more dopamine, there will be reward response.

38 (a) classical conditioning; (b) social learning; (c) operant conditioning.

39 Nicotine is associated with a pleasure response. Cues are associated with nicotine/smoking and give the pleasure response. If someone is exposed to cues without the pleasure response, that should extinguish the association. Someone can be in a bar (with cues) and not turn to smoking.

40 (1) Vicarious reinforcement can be used, where someone is shown to be rewarded for giving up a drug in some way, such as not smoking, and the behaviour is copied because it was rewarded. (2) A role model can be used, someone likely to be a role model for the target group, such as a young sporting hero for young people to look up to and copy. (3) There has to be motivation to change, so showing how to change the behaviour and giving reasons (such as alleviating a heart attack and so not leaving a young family without a parent) can be motivational.

41 (1) Pavlov used dogs when developing classical conditioning and found they salivated to a lab assistant who brought them food, not just to the food. (2) Olds and Milner (1954) stimulated different brain regions and watched when the rat pressed for such stimulation. When the rats pressed for stimulation, the researchers assumed this was the area for pleasure in the brain.

42 The participants are randomly allocated to the treatment or the control group, which can be waiting list or placebo, and that means there is no bias in the allocation and the two groups should match enough to be comparable.

43 The control group is there to give a baseline measure to show what would have happened without the treatment, for example.

44 Interviewing gathers rich qualitative data and, if unstructured, can go with the interviewee to find out about their emotions, attitudes and so on regarding drug usage. Lab experiments have firm controls and gather quantitative data and would not have such rich informative and detailed information to look at issues like individual differences.

45 (1) Olds and Milner (1954) used animals and Pengpid et al. (2013) used human participants. (2) Olds and Milner used careful controls such as precisely where the stimulation was focused in the brain and Pengpid et al. used controls too, such as randomising their participants into the groups so that participant variables were controlled for. (3) Olds and Milner (1954) might find it hard to generalise from rat brains to human brain structures and Pengpid et al. (2013) researched in one culture, using one session of a brief intervention, so generalising might be hard for them too.

Glossary

This section contains definitions of the key terms that you need to know for the topics covered in this book: clinical psychology, criminological psychology, child psychology and health psychology. They are subdivided into each area.

Clinical psychology

Case study in-depth and detailed examination of one person or a small group.

Catastrophising part of CBT and referring to thinking and worrying about what might happen in the future. As this has not yet happened, it is not helpful to worry.

Cognitive triad part of the cognitive model of depression, which is about having a negative view of the self, the world and the future.

Cross-cultural data data that are collected across different cultures to compare them.

Cross-sectional data data that are collected from different groups at one moment in time; they can be different ages to compare development, for example.

Danger one of the 4 'D's of diagnosis, meaning danger to self and/or others.

Delusions a positive symptom of schizophrenia such as when a person believes someone is persecuting them because they are famous — something not borne out by reality.

Deviance one of the 4 'D's of diagnosis, meaning someone's behaviour goes against social norms and in a way that is disapproved of.

Disordered thinking a symptom of schizophrenia when someone finds it hard to put their thoughts into an order that makes sense.

Distress one of the 4 'D's of diagnosis, meaning someone is distressed and that is part of their symptoms, which must be taken into account.

Dizygotic (DZ) twins that are non-identical, coming from two eggs and only sharing 50% of their genes, as would any other sibling. They can be different genders.

Dopamine a neurotransmitter involved in reward and pleasure centres in the brain; excess of it appears to be an explanation for schizophrenia.

DSM the *Diagnostic and Statistical Manual of Mental Disorders*, published by the APA, to give a mental disorder diagnosis.

Dysfunction one of the 4 'D's of diagnosis, meaning behaviours and feelings interfere with someone's ability to function in their lives, such as in their relationships.

Generalising moving from a specific sample's results to say that the results are true of others.

Glutamate a neurotransmitter which is very important in normal brain functioning.

Grounded theory a way of analysing qualitative data, meaning theory is not used to derive categories for analysis but comes from the data themselves.

Hallucinations a positive symptom of schizophrenia referring to seeing or hearing something that is not there.

Inter-rater reliability when two or more raters independently agree in their scoring or assessment.

Interviews a way of gathering data by someone asking questions. Interviews can be either fully structured with a questionnaire to administer, unstructured where there can be probing or semi-structured.

Longitudinal data data that are collected from the same people over time and development can be charted.

Meta-analysis when researchers use other studies and merge them to pool data.

Monozygotic (MZ) twins that are identical, coming from one fertilised egg and sharing 100% of their genes. They are always the same gender.

Neuroimaging a procedure that involves various techniques to image the workings and structure of the nervous system — it is the brain that is focused on in clinical psychology. PET, fMRI and CT scanning are all neuroimaging.

Neurosis refers to mental distress but does not stop daily functioning or thinking rationally as psychosis does.

Neurotransmitters chemicals in the brain involved in messaging. They send signals across the synapse from the pre-synaptic neuron to the post-synaptic neuron.

Primary data data gathered first hand by the researcher.

Psychosis, relating to mental disorder, refers to where someone has lost their sense of reality and their ability to function normally.

Qualitative data data looking at quality and detail, such as people's attitudes and feelings.

Quantitative data data in the form of numbers, such as percentages or number of words recalled.

Reliability refers to data that are consistent because a test is somehow done again and the same results are found.

Schizophrenia a mental disorder characterised by difficulties with thinking, such as disordered thinking, delusions, hallucinations and thought insertion. It affects about one in 100 people.

Secondary data data used by the researcher but which have already been collected by someone else.

Self-report data data provided where someone gives information about themselves using questionnaire or interview.

Glossary

Single-blind technique when the person involved does not know the hypothesis or what is expected.

Social desirability when someone gives an answer that they think they should give to fit with social norms.

Subjectivity when a researcher or clinician brings their own views into a study or into diagnosis. Can be seen as bias.

Thematic analysis a way of analysing qualitative data meaning categories can come from theory or theory can come from the analysis. It means grouping such data.

Thought insertion a symptom of schizophrenia referring to a person thinking someone else is putting thoughts into their head.

Validity refers to data that are about real life and what is said to be measured is what is being measured.

Criminological psychology

Antisocial behaviour refers to behaviour against social norms and where someone's behaviour affects someone else negatively but it might not be against the law.

Case formulation an explanation based both on the information from the assessment of a client and on theory, from which a treatment plan can be derived.

Case study in-depth and detailed examination of one person or a small group.

Cognitive interview four techniques are used: starting from different places for the narrative, giving all the details even if they don't seem important, describing from someone else's viewpoint and imagining the situation to reinstate it in the mind.

Confounding variables variables that have affected the results and have affected any change in the dependent variable.

Credibility refers to data that have been gathered using sufficient controls so there is no bias and the data can be added to a body of knowledge. Credibility is also about trusting the researcher's expertise and there not being subjective bias in the results of a study.

Crime an action or someone not doing something that is an offence and against the law.

Dependent variable (DV) the variable that is measured as a result of manipulation of the independent variable, such as the estimate of speed as a result of manipulating whether the verb is 'smashed' or 'hit'.

Ethics issues of morality in a culture, giving guidelines about what is acceptable and what is not acceptable both in research and in psychology in practice.

Extraneous variables variables that need to be controlled to avoid them affecting the results in an experiment.

Field experiment when controls of an experiment and manipulation of the IV and DV are present but the artificial controlled environment is not.

Hypothesis a statement of what researchers want to find out in a study, a proposed explanation to be tested.

Independent variable (IV) the variable that is manipulated to see its effect, such as whether a verb is 'smashed' or 'hit'.

Labelling giving someone a label that can be about crime, such as 'thief', which affects the person's self-esteem and self-identity as well as giving stigma.

Laboratory experiment there are careful controls over all extraneous variables, an IV is manipulated and a DV measured, so that there are no confounding variables and it can be claimed that the change in the IV caused the change in the DV. Even the setting is controlled, hence the term 'laboratory'.

Mock jury trials experiments where participants are set up as jurors in order to test juror decision-making without using a real trial.

Objectivity means no interpretation from a researcher and no interference from subjective bias.

Operationalised variables have to be made measurable, such as estimate of speed in miles per hour.

Opportunity sampling when the researcher takes whoever is available at the time, which leads to bias in the sample.

Participant variables variables in the person, such as their age, gender, job or upbringing.

Post-event information information that is heard or seen after an event that can affect how someone remembers an event.

Pre-trial publicity information about a defendant and crime that jurors read/hear about before they become a member of the jury for the trial.

Random sampling when each participant has the same chance of being chosen to be in the sample. This is the best as regards least bias.

Reliability refers to data that are consistent because a test is somehow done again and the same results are found.

Self-fulfilling prophecy when someone who is given a negative label and is treated differently because of their label, which can become internalised, feels they cannot change and the prophecy becomes fulfilled.

Situational variables variables in the situation, such as time of day or noise in each condition being different.

Stratified sampling when participants are chosen to suit certain strata or categories in numbers to represent that characteristic in the population.

Temperament aspects of personality that are innate.

Weapon focus when there is a weapon in a scene it holds someone's attention to the extent that other information cannot be well described.

XYY refers to a male with an additional Y chromosome at birth, so having 47 chromosomes.

Child psychology

Ambivalent insecure/anxious resistant Ainsworth's attachment type showing the child stays close to the mother in the Strange Situation and is very distressed when the mother leaves. The child wants to be comforted when the mother returns but rejects the comforting.

Attachment refers to how a child forms a strong bond with another person that tends to be a two-way bond.

Autism at the severe end of autism spectrum disorder, characterised by difficulty with communication and with relationships with others.

Avoidant insecure/anxious avoidant Ainsworth's attachment type showing a child is not distressed when their mother leaves in the Strange Situation and avoids the mother on her return. The child plays normally including when just the stranger is present.

Closed questions where a respondent is constrained in the answer by being given a forced choice.

Covert observations where the participants are not aware that they are part of an observation study.

Cross-cultural data data that are collected across different cultures to compare them.

Day care when a child is cared for by someone other than their parents for some part of the day. It tends to mean a child being in full-time nursery or with a childminder.

Demand characteristics when someone responds in a questionnaire or an interview according to what they think the research requires — a form of bias.

Deprivation refers to attachment and losing a once-formed attachment with poor consequences for a child.

Despair the second of three stages when a child's attachment breaks. They go quiet and withdrawn and lose interest.

Detachment the third of three stages when a child's attachment breaks. They interact with others and seem to show more interest but reject the attachment figure on return and the apparent recovery hides problems.

Disorganised insecure/disoriented added later to Ainsworth's types and meaning a child both approaches the mother on her return and avoids her. The child can dissociate from the situation and feel detached, so their attachment is 'disorganised'.

High systematising being able to use internal rules such as sorting into groups, related to theory of mind and autism.

Internal working model Bowlby's idea that attachment experiences lead an infant to form an internal model of what relationships between people are like and they use those experiences for later relationships.

Low empathising not being able to understand the feelings of others, related to theory of mind and autism.

Maternal deprivation hypothesis Bowlby's claim that a child deprived of attachment with the mother or caregiver can become a juvenile delinquent when older.

Open questions where a respondent can answer using their own words and giving what data they choose.

Overt observations where the participants know about the observation taking place.

Participant observations where the person gathering the data has a role in the situation being observed.

Privation refers to attachment and not having ever formed an attachment, with negative consequences for the child.

Protest the first of three stages when a child's attachment breaks. They protest loudly, crying and looking for the attachment figure.

Safe base Ainsworth's idea that the mother is a safe base from which to explore, if the child is securely attached.

Secure attachment Ainsworth's attachment type that seems to be universally the most likely. The child is distressed when the mother leaves and wants comfort from her when she returns. The mother is a safe base and the child is showing separation anxiety.

Semi-structured interview involves a slightly tighter schedule than an unstructured interview though can divert from the strict set of questions in a structured interview as there is a fairly open framework.

Sensitive mothering Ainsworth said that sensitive mothers, sensitive to their child's needs, tended to have what she called 'securely attached' children.

Separation anxiety Ainsworth's idea that a securely attached child shows anxiety when separated from their attachment figure.

Social desirability when someone gives an answer that they think they should give to fit with social norms — a bias.

Strange Situation procedure Ainsworth's structured observation where an infant's behaviour was recorded. The procedure involved the mother and a stranger going in and out of the room where the infant was. It was the mother's return following the child being left with the stranger that was of interest.

Structured interview when there are set questions to get answers to.

Tallying making a mark when a relevant behaviour is observed and the marks can then be counted.

Theory of mind being able to understand that others have different knowledge than you; a cognitive explanation of autism.

Universals/universality refer to characteristics that are found in all cultures and, therefore, thought to be down to human nature and not to nurture.

Unstructured interview when there is a general schedule to follow but the interviewer can go with the interviewee's thoughts and direction.

Health psychology

Addiction being physically and psychologically dependent on a drug so it becomes all-encompassing.

Aversion therapy a therapy resting on classical conditioning principles where a previously pleasurable response to a stimulus becomes an unpleasant response because of pairing the 'pleasure-producing' stimulus with something that gives an unpleasant response.

CBT cognitive behaviour therapy looks at behaviour using systems such as sticking with anxiety up to a certain amount so that behaviour that is feared can be found to be not so frightening and systems focusing on unhelpful thinking such as catastrophising.

Classical conditioning a stimulus naturally produces a response (such as a drug affects dopamine in the reward pathways and there is a pleasure response). If the stimulus is then paired with a neutral stimulus (such as the drug being paired with related environmental cues) then the new stimulus (e.g. the cues) can bring the pleasure response directly.

Confounding variables variables that were not controlled for and so had an effect on the result of a study (an effect on the dependent variable), other than the independent variable.

Control group the participants getting the condition that does not have the treatment part of the independent variable. This gives a baseline measure.

Control what is put in place to make sure that nothing in an experiment varies except for the IV and the DV.

Dependent variable (DV) the variable that is measured as a result of manipulation of the independent variable, such as the self-reported judgement of effectiveness of CBT.

Dopamine a neurotransmitter that has a role, among other roles, of giving pleasure in the reward pathways of the brain.

Double-blind procedure when neither the participant nor the person running the study knows whether a participant is in the placebo or the treatment group, for example.

Independent variable (IV) the variable that is manipulated to see its effect, such as whether CBT is used as a treatment or whether someone is in a control group.

Neurotransmitters chemicals that pass messages from terminal buttons on the pre-synaptic neuron to receptor sites in the post-synaptic neuron, such as dopamine and serotonin.

Operant conditioning we behave again in a way that was rewarded and we stop doing something if the act was punished.

Physical dependency the body and brain get used to a drug and it can become necessary for 'normal' functioning.

Placebo a sugar pill or something similar so that between a treatment and a control group everything is equal and the same except for the independent variable (e.g. drug vs sugar pill).

Psychological dependency when the emotional and motivational factors of drug taking become part of normal living for a person, and when withdrawal symptoms include loss of motivation, for example.

Randomised controlled trials (RCTs) where participants are randomly allocated to either a treatment or a waiting list/placebo condition to give representative sampling and to make sure the two groups match except for the independent variable.

Receptor sites the post-synaptic neuron has receptors ready to receive certain neurotransmitters and if there is a 'fit' then the message continues.

Semi-structured interview involves a slightly tighter schedule than an unstructured interview though can divert from the strict set of questions in a structured interview as there is a fairly open framework.

Single-blind procedure when the participant does not know whether they are in the placebo or the treatment group, for example.

Social learning we copy those around us, perhaps particularly when we see them rewarded for their behaviour.

Structured interview when there are set questions to get answers to.

Synaptic transmission neurotransmitters are released from the terminal buttons of a pre-synaptic neuron into the synapse, which is a gap. If the receptors on the post-synaptic neuron receive the neurotransmitters (chemicals), the message continues. If not then the message is blocked.

Tolerance when a drug is first taken there will be a quick 'high' but after a while the body habituates and more of the drug is needed to get that same response. This need is called 'tolerance'.

Treatment group the participants getting the treatment part of the independent variable.

Unstructured interview when there is a general schedule to follow but the interviewer can go with the interviewee's thoughts and direction.

Withdrawal when a drug is stopped, there are physical symptoms called 'withdrawal' symptoms, such as dizziness and headaches, and psychological symptoms, such as anxiety and loss of pleasure in things.

Index

Index

J
jury decision-making 29–30

K
key question
    child psychology 45–46
    clinical psychology 21–22
    criminological psychology
       33–34
    health psychology 55–56

L
labelling 26
laboratory experiments 31, 53
learning theories 50, 52–53
longitudinal studies 19

M
maternal deprivation hypothesis 37
mental health *see* clinical
    psychology
meta-analysis 19, 44
methods
    child psychology 42–45
    clinical psychology 18–20
    criminological psychology
       30–33
    health psychology 53–55
monoamine hypothesis 15

N
nature–nurture issues 41, 44, 54
neuroimaging 13
neurotransmitters
    drug addiction 49, 56
    schizophrenia 12–13, 16, 21
    unipolar depression 15, 17

O
objectivity 31
observation 42
offender treatments 27–28
open questions 43
operant conditioning 50

P
personality 25–26
physical dependency 49
placebo 54
post-event information 29
practical investigation
    child psychology 46–47
    clinical psychology 22
    criminological psychology 34
    health psychology 56
pre-trial publicity 30
privation 38, 39
psychological dependency 49
psychosis *see* schizophrenia

Q
qualitative and quantitative data
    20, 43
questionnaires 43

R
randomised controlled trials (RCTs)
    54
receptor sites 49, 50
reliability 10, 11, 31

S
sampling techniques 31, 43
schizophrenia 12–14
    treatments 16–17

self-fulfilling prophecy 26
smoking
    encouraging cessation 55–56
    nicotine addiction 50, 52
social causation hypothesis 14
social desirability 43
social learning 50, 52
Strange Situation procedure 37, 41, 45
studies
    child psychology 45
    clinical psychology 20–21
    criminological psychology 33
    health psychology 55

T
tallying 43
temperament 25–26, 39, 42
theory of mind 41
thought insertion 12
tolerance 48
twin studies 13–14, 39

U
unipolar depression 15–16
    treatments 17–18
universality 41, 44, 45

V
validity 10–11, 12, 31
variables 30

W
weapon focus 29
withdrawal 49

X
XYY syndrome 25